THE GARDENER'S KITCHEN

THE GARDENER'S KITCHEN

A Guide for Preparing Fresh Vegetables

JOHN and GRACE CORRY

WINCHESTER PRESS
Tulsa, Oklahoma

Library of Congress Cataloging in Publication Data

Corry, John, 1948-
The gardener's kitchen.

Includes index.
1. Cookery (vegetables) I. Corry, Grace, 1948-
joint author. II. Title.
TX801.C65   641.6′5   80-18877
ISBN 0-87691-321-4

Published by Winchester Press
1421 South Sheridan
P. O. Box 1260
Tulsa, Oklahoma 74101

Book Design by Quentin Fiore
Printed in the United States
1 2 3 4 5   84 83 82 81 80

CONTENTS

INTRODUCTION

In 1973 we took up vegetable gardening—along with three or four million other Americans. The early 1970s was when America's backyard renaissance began. That rebirth is still unfolding; each year, people in this country discover the joys of gardening for the first time, adding to the massive numbers of people who have made the discovery in preceding years. As we begin the 1980s, there are, according to the United States Department of Agriculture, nearly 50 million home gardeners in this country, all of them motivated to cut their food costs as much as possible—but also motivated to derive the keen satisfaction that comes from raising at least a part of their own food.

We suffered the usual hardships that first spring, as do most people who finally get tired of looking at so much lawn and decide their yards—or at least part of their yards—would serve them much better if they could be counted on to produce some food. We suffered the blisters, sore backs, and grubby nails, and the insects (on the wing and on the crawl) which came to wreak senseless damage on our tender—our first!—vegetables. We battled with rabbits and gophers. We found our first scarecrow awesome (alas, the grackles and starlings were not so impressed). Early evenings, straining our eyes in the failing light, we swatted away mosquito swarms as we labored to plant just one more row of peas, or clear just another square foot of ground of weeds. What gardeners' obstacles we didn't overcome, we at least became inured to.

At harvest time, though, we were confronted by a problem that couldn't necessarily be overcome with just labor or will. What to do with our crops? How to cook them? There were lots of vegetable recipes in the cookbooks in our kitchen library, but for the most part, we decided, they were the wrong kind.

The recipes failed on at least one of the following counts (and most of them, we still believe, failed on *all* counts). They were too complicated, there were too many steps in the recipes, they required too many utensils, they took too long, and they often called for "exotic" ingredients and condiments. They were either unavailable in our part of rural Pennsylvania, or, if they were available, they were so costly that buying them negated the whole idea of having an economical garden.

Harvest time of that first gardening season was when we started working on this book. But we worked on *The Gardener's Kitchen* for quite a while before we realized it was going to really be a book. All we were really concerned about, in the beginning, was collecting recipes that would be practical, quick, and easy to make—and not calling for any more extra ingredients than you would expect to find in even the most nominally stocked

7

kitchen. We believed we were looking for a reasonable compromise; since we'd already invested so much labor in our garden, we didn't want to spend undue amounts of further labor in turning out our dishes.

So we put out the word to friends, neighbors, and relatives. Some of the people who lived on our rarely traveled dirt road—people who had been gardening since the 1930s—were most helpful. Also very helpful were relatives and friends we wrote to. Recipes came in from all over the country. Slowly, through trial and error, *The Gardener's Kitchen* evolved. Along with developing several recipes of our own, we had to test all of the recipes submitted to us (many were rejected, not because they were unpalatable, but because they were just too much work—or they simply weren't special enough).

After several seasons of gardening and testing, we had our cookbook complete. If there is a philosophy here, it is that fresh vegetables are versatile. Certain recipes can stand as a meal in themselves. Other recipes can be accompaniments to meat, fish, or fowl main dishes (or even to vegetable main dishes). *The Gardener's Kitchen* is for those cook/gardeners who want to take freshly harvested vegetables directly from the garden and into the kitchen where they can be turned into exciting, nourishing dishes in a short period of time and with the littlest possible effort. We have included at least a few recipes on each of the most common vegetables—the ones which can be grown in virtually every part of the country by just about everybody. Those vegetables that seem to get produced in profusion, like tomatoes and zucchini squashes, have many recipes devoted to them. Of course, this book is also for nongardeners who are looking for special ways to prepare vegetables.

The Gardener's Kitchen has been written to fill a gap. It is a bridge between strictly vegetarian-style cooking and the gourmet method. It is for everyone who loves fresh vegetables, but it is particularly for those who have their own gardens—or at least those who have easy access to fresh vegetables.

JOHN and GRACE CORRY

COOKING NOTES

In addition to gathering a collection of vegetable recipes which could be made easily and quickly, we set an additional criterion: the utensils should be found in nearly every kitchen. The recipes in *The Gardener's Kitchen* have been standardized as much as possible. The methods and steps are few in number and similar in all recipes. Every recipe here can be made with *only six* different sizes of utensils:

1. Small saucepan (1-quart capacity)
2. Large saucepan (3-quart capacity)
3. Skillet or small skillet (8 or 9 in. in diameter)
4. Large skillet (12 in. in diameter)
5. Shallow casserole or shallow baking dish (1-quart capacity)
6. Deep casserole or deep baking dish (2½-quart capacity)

Quick-cooking Vegetables

For an easy, fast way to enjoy fresh vegetables, use the quick-cook methods detailed in Chapter One. After cooking a vegetable using this method, season to taste with salt and pepper and butter or margarine. **Note:** When a recipe calls for a certain amount of a vegetable *cooked*, use the quick-cook method.

Pressure-cooking Vegetables

If you own a pressure cooker, you already know what a time-saver it can be. In fact, pressure cooking just about anything takes about 1/3 of the time that other methods require (this includes from the time the lid is put on the cooker until the release of the built up pressure). We recommend pressure-cooking vegetables at 15 pounds of pressure. Check the gauge on your cooker for accuracy at least once a year.

It is absolutely necessary that you observe the manufacturer's instructions for your particular pressure cooker in regards to safety, amount of liquid to be used, and operating instructions. Always use seasonings sparingly in a pressure cooker.

Pressure-cooking vegetables does more than save time for the cook, of course — it is perhaps the best way to preserve flavors and keep the loss of nutrients to a minimum. Try pressure-cooking vegetables with a steaming rack, also. The rack stands on 1-inch pegs (to keep vegetables above the liquid) and expands to fit almost every size cooker. When steaming vegetables in a pressure cooker, cook for 1–2 minutes longer than you would without the rack.

Meat, Fish, Fowl

This is a vegetable cookbook, but it is not a vegetarian cookbook. Feel free to dress up many of the recipes in the collection with meats, fish, or chicken. Here are a few suggestions for you to try.

1. Add canned fishes—tuna, anchovies, chopped sardines, etc.—to cold salads.

2. Add fish and shellfish to white stock soups. Sauté filets, then drop boneless pieces into soups in the last 2–3 minutes of simmering. Add fresh, cooked clams, mussels, or oysters and their juices to soups in the last 1–2 minutes of simmering.

3. Add chicken to white stock soups. The chicken should be cooked using any method but deep frying, then diced or shredded and added in the last 5 minutes of simmering.

4. Try pork or lamb chops on casseroles and combination dishes. Fry the chops in a hot skillet until browned well (cook the pork chops at least 8 minutes per each side—even longer if chops are thick), then place them on top of the casserole or combination dish and bake them with the vegetables.

5. Add beef chunks to stews, casseroles, combination dishes, and brown stock soups. For soups, cut or slice beef in smaller pieces than you would for the other dishes. One-inch chunks should be the largest size pieces; however, always dredge the beef in flour, place the pieces in a sieve and shake off excess flour, then fry in oil until well-browned and drain. Add the beef to brown stock soups for the entire length of simmering. For stews, casseroles, and combination dishes, stir in beef chunks and cook for the entire simmering or baking period.

6. Ground beef, browned by frying, is excellent stirred into casseroles, stews, and combination dishes. Be sure to drain it thoroughly before adding it to any dish. With casseroles, try ground beef as a topping, spreading it across the casserole during the last 10 minutes of baking.

VEGETABLES

ASPARAGUS

Preparing
If the thick ends of the asparagus stalks are tough, gently bend them until the ends break off. Remove the scales with a knife and scrub the stalks with a gentle brush, rinsing under cold water.

Quick-cook method
Place stalks or pieces in a large skillet, sprinkle with salt, and pour boiling water to cover over the asparagus. Bring to a boil, then reduce heat and simmer, covered, for 5 minutes or until tender; drain.

ASPARAGUS VINAIGRETTE

1 pound asparagus, cooked and drained
6 tablespoons vegetable oil
2 tablespoons vinegar
2 teaspoons mild prepared mustard
½ teaspoon sugar
⅛ teaspoon salt
pepper to taste

Combine last 6 ingredients in a small saucepan and cook, stirring frequently, over low heat until well blended (do this while asparagus is cooking). Drain asparagus and pour heated sauce over it. Serve at once. Serves 4.

ASPARAGUS PIE

2 pounds asparagus, cut into 1-inch pieces, cooked and drained
3 tablespoons butter or margarine
3 tablespoons flour
1 cup milk
1 chicken bouillon cube, crushed
1 teaspoon minced onion
½ teaspoon salt
pepper to taste
⅓ cup grated Cheddar cheese
4 hard-cooked eggs, chopped
9-inch pastry shell, baked

Melt butter in a large saucepan and blend in flour; add milk and cook over low heat, stirring constantly until thickened. Add bouillon cube, onion, salt, and pepper; stir until bouillon is dissolved. Remove from heat and add asparagus and eggs; blend well. Turn mix into pie shell and bake at 350°F for 10 minutes. Serve at once.

BAKED ASPARAGUS WITH SOUR CREAM

1 pound asparagus, cooked and drained
⅔ cup dairy sour cream
½ cup butter or margarine
2⅓ cups soft bread crumbs
½ teaspoon salt

Place asparagus spears in the bottom of a shallow, buttered baking dish. Spread the sour cream evenly over the spears. In a large saucepan, melt butter over low heat, then add bread crumbs and salt and mix together. Sprinkle bread crumbs over sour cream and bake at 375°F for 20 minutes or until top is browned. Serves 4.

ASPARAGUS PARMESAN

2 pounds asparagus
⅓ cup flour
1 egg, beaten well with 1 tablespoon cold water
3 tablespoons grated Parmesan cheese
1 cup seasoned bread crumbs
1 teaspoon salt
⅛ teaspoon pepper
olive or vegetable oil

Cut off and discard any tough asparagus ends. Dip stalks in flour, then in egg, and last into a mixture of the cheese, bread crumbs, salt, and pepper. In a large skillet, fry stalks in hot oil (375°F) for 10 minutes or until tender. Serves 4 to 6.

ASPARAGUS RING

2 cups asparagus tips, cooked and drained
3 tablespoons butter or margarine
3 tablespoons flour
½ teaspoon salt
1 cup sweet cream
3 egg yolks, beaten well
3 egg whites, beaten stiffly

In a small saucepan, melt butter and blend in flour and salt; add cream over low heat, stirring constantly until smooth. Put egg yolks in a large saucepan and pour butter–cream mixture over them; stir a few times; cool. Fold in egg whites and asparagus tips. Turn mixture into a 2-quart buttered ring mold, set in a pan of hot water, and bake at 350°F for 30 minutes or until set. Serves 4 to 6.

CHEDDARED ASPARAGUS

1 pound asparagus, cut into 1-inch pieces, cooked and drained
5 tablespoons butter or margarine
¼ cup flour
½ teaspoon salt
pepper to taste
1 cup grated mild Cheddar cheese

In a large saucepan, melt butter, then blend in flour; add milk, salt, and pepper and cook over low heat, stirring constantly until thick. Add cheese and stir until blended smoothly. Add asparagus, mix well, and cook over low heat for 5 minutes. Serves 4.

ONION-DRESSED ASPARAGUS

1 pound asparagus, cut into 1-inch pieces, cooked and drained
3 tablespoons melted butter or margarine
2 tablespoons onion, minced
1 tablespoon vinegar
1 teaspoon sugar
½ teaspoon salt
dash paprika

Mix dressing ingredients thoroughly. Pour over hot asparagus and serve at once. Serves 4.

ASPARAGUS BAKE

2 cups asparagus tips, cooked and drained
2 tablespoons butter or margarine
2 tablespoons flour
1 cup milk
½ teaspoon salt
⅛ teaspoon pepper
4 eggs, beaten well

Line the bottom of a standard, buttered loaf pan with 1 cup of the asparagus tips; rub the other cup of tips through a coarse sieve; set aside. Melt the butter in a small saucepan and blend in the flour, salt, and pepper; add the milk slowly, cooking over low heat and stirring constantly until smooth; add the eggs and blend thoroughly; add sieved asparagus and blend. Pour mixture into the loaf pan, place the pan in a pan of hot water, and bake for 45 minutes at 350°F. Serves 4 to 6.

BEANS
Green, Wax, Lima

Preparing
Snap off bean ends and remove any strings. Rinse in cool water. Limas should be shelled, like peas, and not washed.

Quick-cook method
In a covered saucepan, cook quantity of green or wax beans, sliced in any style, in boiling, salted water until tender; drain. Cook limas in boiling, salted water to cover in a covered saucepan until tender, at least 10 minutes; drain.

BEAN SHUFFLE AND SOUR CREAM
½ pound green beans, cut into 1-inch pieces
½ pound yellow (wax) beans, cut into 1-inch pieces
2 tablespoons chopped chives
5 tablespoons vegetable oil
1 tablespoon flour
1 tablespoon cold water
salt and pepper to taste
⅔ cup dairy sour cream

In a large skillet, fry beans in hot oil (375°F) for 3 minutes, turning frequently. Add chives, flour, water, salt, pepper, and sour cream and blend all thoroughly. Turn mixture into a shallow baking dish and bake at 350°F for 15 minutes. Serves 4.

SWEET-AND-SOUR BEANS
½ pound green beans, cut into 1-inch pieces, cooked and drained
½ pound yellow (wax) beans, cut into 1-inch pieces, cooked and
    drained
3 tablespoons butter or margarine
¼ teaspoon salt
3 tablespoons cold water
2 tablespoons sugar
1 teaspoon cornstarch
2 tablespoons vinegar
1 tablespoon soy sauce

In a large saucepan, melt butter, then add beans and cook, covered, over very low heat, for 2 minutes. Mix remainder of ingredients until well blended, then pour over beans. Raise heat to medium, and cook uncovered, stirring frequently, for 5 minutes. Serves 4.

SAUCED BEANS

½ pound green beans, cut into 1-inch pieces
½ pound yellow (wax) beans, cut into 1-inch pieces
1 tablespoon minced onion
3 tablespoons butter or margarine
½ cup warm water
salt and pepper to taste
⅓ cup warm evaporated milk

Melt butter in a large skillet; add beans, onion, water, salt and pepper and cook covered over very low heat until tender. Remove cover, raise heat to medium, add milk, mixing well, and cook 2 minutes. Serves 4.

HERBY'S HERBY BEANS

½ pound green beans, cut into 1-inch pieces, cooked and drained
½ pound yellow (wax) beans, cut into 1-inch pieces, cooked and
    drained
3 tablespoons minced onion
3 tablespoons minced celery
1 small clove garlic, minced
5 tablespoons butter or margarine
½ teaspoon salt
dash marjoram
½ teaspoon dried rosemary
½ teaspoon dried basil

While beans are cooking, melt butter in a small saucepan; add onion, garlic, and celery and cook over low heat until tender. Stir in salt, marjoram, rosemary, and basil. Pour sauce over hot beans, toss a few times, and serve at once. Serves 4.

ITALIAN-STYLE GREEN BEANS

1 pound green beans, cut into 1-inch pieces, cooked and drained
1 small onion, chopped
1 small clove garlic, minced
2 tablespoons olive or vegetable oil
½ teaspoon sugar
salt and pepper to taste
oregano

In a large saucepan, fry garlic in hot oil for 1 minute. Add chopped onion and fry until tender. Toss green beans with sugar, salt, and pepper, then add to skillet. Fry beans over high heat until just beginning to brown. Drain off part of liquid, sprinkle with oregano, and serve at once. Serves 4.

GREEN BEANS PARMESAN

1 pound green beans, cut into 1-inch pieces, cooked and drained
1 small onion, chopped
3 tablespoons butter or margarine
1 tablespoon flour
½ teaspoon salt
pepper to taste
dash marjoram
⅔ cup milk
½ cup grated Parmesan cheese

Melt butter in a large saucepan and cook onion until tender. Add flour and blend until smooth. Add salt, pepper, marjoram, and milk; raise heat to medium and cook, stirring constantly, until smooth; add cheese and cook, stirring constantly, until smooth. Add hot beans, stir a few times, and serve at once. Serves 4.

GREEN BEANS AND BACON

1½ pounds green beans, cut into 1-inch pieces, cooked and drained
2 slices bacon
⅛ teaspoon onion juice
salt and pepper to taste

Fry bacon in a large skillet until well-done; break strips into small pieces. Add beans, onion juice, salt, and pepper and stir all together. Fry over medium heat 5 minutes. Serve at once. Serves 4 to 6.

SASSY GREEN BEANS

½ pound green beans, cut into 1-inch pieces, cooked, drained, and cooled
½ pound yellow (wax) beans, cut into 1-inch pieces, cooked, drained, and cooled
1 small clove garlic
1 tablespoon salt
1 teaspoon dill weed
1 teaspoon mustard seed
1 cup white vinegar
¾ cup water
⅓ cup sugar
⅛ teaspoon cayenne pepper

Combine all ingredients except beans in a large saucepan, bring to a boil, reduce heat, and simmer 10 minutes; cool. Place beans in a shallow casserole, pour liquid over, stir a few times, and cover; refrigerate overnight before serving. Serve cold. Serves 4.

CREAMED LIMAS

1½ pounds limas, cooked and drained
1 tablespoon chopped chives
salt and pepper to taste
2 tablespoons butter or margarine
3 tablespoons milk
3 tablespoons evaporated milk
3 tablespoons grated mild Cheddar cheese

Toss beans, chives, salt, and pepper thoroughly; set aside. Melt butter in a large saucepan, then add milk and evaporated milk, stirring until smooth. Raise heat to medium, add cheese, and cook, stirring constantly, until smooth. Add hot limas, stir a few times, and serve at once. Serves 4 to 6.

LEANNA'S LIMAS WITH SCALLIONS

1 pound limas, cooked and drained
3 scallions, sliced thin
3 tablespoons butter or margarine
1 teaspoon flour
salt and pepper to taste

Melt butter in a large saucepan, then add scallions, stir a few times and simmer, covered, for 3 minutes. Add flour and blend until smooth. Sprinkle hot limas with salt and pepper and add limas to saucepan. Stir a few times, raise heat to medium, and cook 2 minutes. Serve at once. Serves 4.

SPICY LIMAS

1 pound limas, cooked and drained
2 scallions, sliced thin
1 tablespoon butter or margarine
2 tablespoons warm water
1 tablespoon olive oil
⅛ teaspoon cayenne pepper
dash salt
dash pepper

Melt butter in a large saucepan, then add scallions and cook over low heat for 1 minute. Add beans and remainder of ingredients, mix thoroughly, and simmer, covered, for 10 minutes. Serves 4.

AUSTRO-HUNGARIAN LIMAS

1 pound limas, cooked and drained
1 teaspoon minced onion
⅓ cup warm water
⅓ cup dairy sour cream
½ teaspoon salt
pepper to taste
¼ teaspoon dry mustard
½ teaspoon Worcestershire sauce

Combine all ingredients at once and mix thoroughly. Turn into a shallow, buttered baking dish and bake at 325°F. for 40 minutes. Serves 4.

CURRIED LIMAS

1 pound limas, cooked and drained
1 tablespoon minced onion
3 tablespoons butter or margarine
1 tablespoon flour
½ cup milk
1 teaspoon curry powder

Melt butter in a large saucepan, then cook onion over low heat for 1 minute. Blend in flour until smooth; add milk and curry powder, raise heat to medium, and cook, stirring constantly, for 3 minutes. Add hot limas, stir a few times, and cook another minute. Serve at once. Serves 4.

BEETS

Preparing
Cut off stems and root tip. Wash and scrub, removing grit and strings. Do not pare.

Quick-cook method
Cook, covered, in boiling, salted water, 30 to 50 minutes, depending on size of beets; beets are done when easily pierced with a fork. Pare when cooled, then slice or dice.

HARVARD BEETS

2 cups beets, cooked, drained, pared, and cubed
1 tablespoon cornstarch
¼ cup vinegar
¼ cup water in which beets were cooked
¼ cup sugar
½ teaspoon salt
3 tablespoons melted butter or margarine

In a large saucepan, combine cornstarch, vinegar, beet water, sugar, and salt; bring to a boil, reduce heat to low, and stir until smooth. Add the beets and simmer, covered, for 15 minutes. Add the melted butter last, stir a few times, and bring to a boil. Serve at once. Serves 4 to 6.

GRANDMA'S GRATED BEETS

1½ cups beets, pared and grated
1 teaspoon chopped chives
5 tablespoons butter or margarine
½ teaspoon salt
pepper to taste

Toss all ingredients except butter together. Melt butter in a large skillet, then add beet mixture. Raise heat to high and fry for 5 minutes, turning frequently. Serves 4.

SPICY BEETS

2 cups beets, cooked, drained, pared, and chopped coarsely
3 tablespoons butter or margarine
1 teaspoon horseradish
½ teaspoon mild prepared mustard
dash garlic salt
⅛ teaspoon white pepper
1 teaspoon white vinegar

Melt butter in a large saucepan, then blend in all ingredients except beets; cook over low heat for 1 minute. Add beets, raise heat to medium, and cook, turning frequently, for 4 minutes. Serve at once. Serves 4 to 6.

SOUR CREAM BEETS

1⅓ cup beets, cooked, drained, pared, and diced
1 tablespoon melted butter or margarine
⅓ cup dairy sour cream
1 tablespoon warm water
1 teaspoon vinegar
½ teaspoon sugar
⅛ teaspoon salt

Blend all ingredients together except the beets in a large saucepan; cook over medium heat, stirring frequently, for 1 minute. Stir in beets and cook, stirring frequently, for 3 minutes. Serve at once. Serves 4 to 6.

UNBEATABLE BEETS

1½ cups beets, cooked, drained, pared, and diced
1 small onion, chopped
3 tablespoons sugar
¼ teaspoon salt
dash white pepper
⅓ cup white vinegar
1 tablespoon cold water
½ cup water in which beets were cooked

Combine all ingredients except beets in a large saucepan and bring to a boil, stirring frequently. Remove from heat, add beets, mix thoroughly, cool, cover, and refrigerate overnight. Serve cold. Serves 4.

BROCCOLI

Preparing
Avoid heads with "spreading" or yellowing flowers. Cut off any oversized or withered outer leaves, then rinse. Cut off any tough parts of stalk, then rinse again, washing flowers thoroughly.

Quick-cook method
Whole head method: If the stalks are larger than 1 inch in diameter, hold the head upside down and, using a sharp knife, slice the stalks almost to the flowers, the slices ¼ inch thick. Cook covered in boiling, salted water until tender, 5 to 10 minutes.

Piece method: Cut stalks into pieces 1-inch long and no wider than ½-inch. Drop into salted, boiling water and cook 5 minutes. Drop flowers into water, cover, and cook another 5 minutes or until flowers are tender.

BROCCOLI AU FROMAGE

1 large head broccoli, cut in pieces, cooked, and drained
3 tablespoons butter or margarine
1 teaspoon cornstarch
1½ cups milk
½ teaspoon salt
pepper to taste
¾ cup grated Cheddar, Parmesan, or Gouda cheese

While broccoli is cooking, melt butter in a small saucepan, then blend in cornstarch, milk, salt, and pepper, stirring until smooth. Raise heat to medium and add cheese gradually, cooking and stirring constantly until smooth and thickened. Serve sauce over hot broccoli spears. Serves 4.

SKILLET-SIMMERED BROCCOLI

1 large head broccoli, chopped coarsely
1 small onion, sliced thin
1 large green pepper, sliced
3 tablespoons warm water
3 tablespoons olive or vegetable oil
½ teaspoon salt
pepper to taste

In a large skillet, simmer onions and pepper in hot oil until tender; add water, salt, pepper, and broccoli and simmer, covered, until just tender. Remove cover, raise heat to high, and fry, turning frequently, until broccoli parts just begin to brown. Serves 4.

BROCCOLI LOAF

1 small head broccoli, cooked, drained, and chopped coarsely
2 scallions, sliced thin
3 tablespoons butter or margarine
2 tablespoons flour
1 cup milk
⅔ cup mayonnaise
3 eggs, beaten well
salt and pepper to taste
dash cayenne pepper

Melt butter in a large saucepan, then blend in flour, stirring until smooth. Raise heat to medium, add milk, salt, pepper, and cayenne, stirring constantly until blended well. Remove from heat and add scallions, mayonnaise, and eggs and blend well. Drop cooked broccoli pieces into a large, greased casserole, then pour mixture over broccoli. Place casserole in a pan of hot water and bake at 350°F for 30 minutes, or until set. Serves 4 to 6.

BROCCOLI PIE

1¾ cups chopped broccoli flowers
½ cup grated broccoli stalk
1 medium onion, chopped
2 tablespoons butter or margarine
1 cup milk
1 teaspoon salt
½ teaspoon pepper
2 eggs, beaten slightly
¾ cup grated mild Cheddar cheese
pastry for bottom of 9-inch piepan

Melt butter in a small saucepan and cook onions over low heat until just tender. Add milk, salt, pepper, and eggs, blending until smooth. Raise heat to medium and add cheese and grated broccoli, stirring constantly until blended; remove from heat. Line bottom of pastry-lined piepan with broccoli flower parts, then pour mixture over. Bake at 350°F for 50 minutes, or until set and lightly browned.

BRUSSELS SPROUTS

Preparing
Choose only heads that are tight and bright green. Cut off stems. Discard any dried or wilted leaves. Rinse thoroughly.

Quick-cook method
Cook whole in a large amount of boiling, salted water, uncovered, for 6 to 10 minutes or until just tender.

HOLIDAY BRUSSELS SPROUTS

1 pound brussels sprouts, halved
½ cup celery, minced
1 tablespoon chopped chives
2 tablespoons butter or margarine
salt and pepper to taste
2 tablespoons grated Parmesan or Cheddar cheese

In a large, covered saucepan, cook brussels sprouts and celery in a small amount of water for 2 minutes over high heat. Remove cover, reduce heat to medium, and continue cooking until sprouts are tender, another 2 to 3 minutes. Remove pan from heat, add chives, butter, salt and pepper, stirring a few times until butter is melted. Top with sprinkled cheese and serve at once. Serves 4.

CREAMED BRUSSELS SPROUTS

1 pound whole brussels sprouts, cooked and drained
3 tablespoons butter or margarine
2 tablespoons flour
½ cup water in which sprouts were cooked
½ cup milk
3 tablespoons heavy cream

Melt butter in a small saucepan, then blend in flour until smooth. Raise heat to medium and add water and milk, stirring constantly until smooth. Remove from heat, fold in cream, then pour mixture over hot brussels sprouts. Serve at once. Serves 4.

LEMONY BRUSSELS SPROUTS

1 pound brussels sprouts, cooked and drained
1 tablespoon butter or margarine
3 tablespoons lemon juice
⅓ cup dairy sour cream
salt and pepper to taste

Melt butter in a large saucepan over low heat, then add lemon juice, sour cream, salt, and pepper, blending all thoroughly. Pour mixture over hot brussels sprouts and serve at once. Serves 4.

MARINATED BRUSSELS SPROUTS

1 pound brussels sprouts, cooked and drained
½ small garlic clove, minced
1 teaspoon chopped chives
3 tablespoons vegetable oil
1 teaspoon dried parsley flakes
¼ teaspoon sugar
¼ teaspoon salt
¼ teaspoon pepper
dash cayenne pepper
2 tablespoons lemon juice
2 tablespoons wine vinegar

Combine all ingredients except lemon juice and vinegar in a large bowl or saucepan, stir a few times, and refrigerate covered overnight. Just before serving, combine lemon juice and vinegar, then sprinkle over the brussels sprouts. serves 4.

CABBAGE

Preparing
Always select heads that are firm and heavy. Remove the first layer of outer leaves. With a sharp knife, cut into the core until all of the tough part is removed. Holding the stem end up, rinse under hot water a few seconds, then rinse thoroughly under cold water.

Quick-cook method
Shred cabbage with a sharp knife into slices ¼ inch to 1 inch wide. Drop slices into boiling, salted water, cover and cook until tender, about 3 to 5 minutes.

CAROLINA BAKED CABBAGE

1 large head cabbage, chopped coarsely
1 teaspoon salt
¼ teaspoon pepper
2 tablespoons melted butter or margarine
2 eggs, beaten lightly
1 tablespoon vinegar
⅓ cup heavy cream

In a large saucepan, cook cabbage in boiling, salted water until just tender; drain. Add remainder of ingredients and mix thoroughly. Turn into a deep, buttered baking dish and bake at 375°F for 25 minutes, or until browned lightly. Serves 6 to 8.

COLORFUL CABBAGE

3 cups cabbage, chopped fine
1 small onion, chopped
1 small green pepper, diced
1 large tomato, diced
¼ cup celery, diced
2 tablespoons water
3 tablespoons butter or margarine
salt and pepper to taste

Combine water and vegetables in a large skillet and cook, covered, over medium heat for 5 minutes. Remove cover and add butter, salt, and pepper. Cook stirring frequently until tender, at least 5 minutes. Serve at once. Serves 4 to 6.

CABBAGE AND SOUR CREAM

6 cups cabbage, chopped fine
1 scallion, sliced thin
2 tablespoons butter or margarine
2 tablespoons warm water
¼ cup dairy sour cream
1 teaspoon sugar
¼ teaspoon salt
1 teaspoon lemon juice

Melt butter in a large skillet and cook scallion over low heat for 3 minutes. Add cabbage and water and cook, covered, over medium heat for 5 minutes. Remove cover, raise heat to high, add remainder of ingredients, stir well, and cook another 3 minutes, stirring frequently. Serve at once. Serves 4 to 6.

CARAWAY CABBAGE

3 cups cabbage, shredded, cooked, drained, and still hot
¼ cup melted butter or margarine
1 teaspoon caraway seeds
1 teaspoon lemon juice
salt and pepper to taste

Combine all ingredients at once in a large bowl and toss until thoroughly mixed. Serve immediately. Serves 4.

CURRIED CABBAGE

1 small head cabbage, shredded, cooked, and drained
1 scallion, sliced thin
3 tablespoons butter or margarine
1 teaspoon curry powder
½ teaspoon sugar
salt and pepper to taste

Melt butter in a large skillet, then add scallion, curry powder, sugar, salt, and pepper; cook over low heat for 5 minutes. Add cabbage, raise heat to high, and cook, turning frequently, for 5 minutes. Serve at once. Serves 4.

CARROTS

Preparing
Simply cut off the top of the carrot, scrub with a vegetable brush under running water, and rinse one final time.

Quick-cook method
Small, young carrots can be cooked whole; more mature carrots should be cut into pieces or sticks. In either a skillet or a saucepan, cook carrots, covered, in just enough salted, boiling water to cover until tender.

GOLDEN GLAZED CARROTS
6 large carrots, slices, cooked, and drained
¼ pound butter or margarine
¼ cup brown sugar, packed

Melt butter in a large skillet, then blend in brown sugar until smooth. Raise heat to medium, add carrots and cook, turning carrots constantly until thoroughly glazed. Serves 4 to 6.

DEEP-FRIED CARROTS
2 dozen small carrots or 1 dozen medium carrots, halved lengthwise, cooked, and drained
milk
½ cup flour
shortening

Dip each carrot piece in milk, then roll it in flour, coating it thoroughly. In a large skillet, in hot shortening (375°F) fry carrots until they are a deep brown. Drain on absorbent paper and serve. Serves 4.

PAN-FRIED CARROTS
3 large carrots, sliced thinly
1 small onion, chopped
1 small green pepper, minced
1 teaspoon water
3 tablespoons butter or margarine
salt and pepper to taste

Melt butter in a large skillet and add water, salt, and pepper. Add vegetables and fry over medium heat until just tender. Serve at once. Serves 4.

CARROTS CAYENNE

4 large carrots, sliced thinly
2 cups boiling water
3 tablespoons butter or margarine
2 tablespoons flour
¾ cup milk
1 teaspoon ground cloves
½ teaspoon salt
1 small bay leaf
dash cayenne pepper

Place carrots, boiling water, cloves, and bay leaf in a large saucepan, cover, and cook over medium heat until carrots are tender; drain, reserving 1 cup of liquid, and set aside. Melt butter in a large saucepan, then blend in flour; raise heat to medium, add milk and 1 cup of liquid, and cook until thickened, stirring frequently. Add carrots, salt, and cayenne and continue cooking for 5 minutes, stirring frequently. Serve at once. Serves 4.

CREAMED CARROTS

3 cups carrots, sliced thinly, cooked and drained
1 tablespoon butter or margarine
salt and pepper to taste
½ teaspoon sugar
½ cup whipping cream

Melt butter in a large skillet and add warm carrots, salt, pepper, and sugar; mix well. Add whipping cream, raise heat to medium, and cook for 5 minutes, stirring frequently. Serve at once. Serves 4.

MARINATED CARROTS

6 large carrots, sliced, cooked, and drained
1 small onion, minced
½ cup olive or vegetable oil
1 tablespoon salt
¼ teaspoon pepper
1 teaspoon sugar
2 tablespoons lemon juice
1 tablespoon white vinegar
1 cup water

Combine all ingredients except carrots in a large saucepan and bring to a boil. Drop carrots in boiling liquid and remove from heat. Allow to cool, then refrigerate overnight. Drain before serving. Serves 4 to 6.

CARROT PATTIES

1 cup carrots, grated
1 teaspoon onion, grated
2 cups unseasoned bread crumbs
¼ teaspoon baking powder
3 tablespoons milk
1 tablespoon water
¼ teaspoon salt
2 eggs, beaten well
butter or margarine

Combine all ingredients except butter and mix thoroughly. Form into thin cakes and cook in melted butter in a hot skillet or griddle until lightly browned on both sides. Serve hot with honey or syrup. Serves 4.

CONTINENTAL CARROTS

3 cups carrots, sliced, cooked, and drained
2 tablespoons green pepper, minced
1 tablespoon scallions, thinly sliced
¼ teaspoon lemon juice
¾ cup dairy sour cream

Combine all ingredients in a large saucepan and mix thoroughly. Cook over medium heat, stirring constantly, for about 5 minutes. Serve at once. Serves 4.

CAULIFLOWER

Preparing
Pick only tight heads that have compact flowers and no yellowish spots. Discard leaves. Rinse thoroughly. Either leave the head whole or cut off the flowers for use and discard the core.

Quick-cook method
Place whole head, flowers, or sliced or chopped flowers in 1 to 1½ inches of boiling, salted water in a large saucepan. Cover and cook until just tender.

CAULIFLOWER COLLAGE

2 cups cauliflower flowers, sliced thinly
1 small green pepper, minced
1 tablespoon butter or margarine
½ cup water
salt and pepper to taste

Melt butter in a large skillet, then add remainder of ingredients. Cook covered over medium-high heat until cauliflower is tender. Serve at once. Serves 4.

FRIED CAULIFLOWER

4 cups cauliflower flowers, sliced thinly
1 teaspoon chopped chives
2 tablespoons water
2 tablespoons butter or margarine
2 tablespoons heavy cream
salt and pepper to taste

Cook the cauliflower in water in a large, covered skillet over medium heat until just tender. Add butter, cream, salt, and pepper. Raise heat to high and fry 3 to 4 minutes, turning frequently. Serve at once. Serves 4.

CAULIFLOWER CHEDDAR

4 cups cauliflower flowers, sliced, cooked, and drained
2 tablespoons butter or margarine
1 teaspoon flour
½ cup grated Cheddar cheese
salt and pepper to taste

Melt butter in a small saucepan, then blend in flour, cheese, salt, and pepper, cooking and stirring over low heat until smooth. Pour sauce over hot cauliflower and serve at once. Serves 4.

CAULIFLOWER SOUFFLÉ

1 large head cauliflower, the flowers removed, sliced, cooked,
        and drained
1 teaspoon chopped chives
3 tablespoons butter or margarine
2 tablespoons flour
1 cup milk
½ cup grated mild Cheddar cheese
¾ cup unseasoned bread crumbs
1 teaspoon salt
¼ teaspoon pepper
2 egg yolks, beaten
2 egg whites, beaten stiffly

Melt butter in a small saucepan and blend in flour; add milk and blend thoroughly; add cheese, bread crumbs, chives, salt, pepper, and egg yolks and cook over medium heat 3 minutes, stirring constantly. Remove from heat and fold in egg whites. Drop cauliflower slices into a deep, buttered baking dish, then pour mixture over them. Place in a pan of hot water and bake at 375°F for 35 minutes or until set. Serves 4 to 6.

CAULIFLOWER PARMESAN

1 large head cauliflower, the flowers removed, cooked, and drained
5 tablespoons butter or margarine
¼ cup seasoned bread crumbs
¼ cup grated Parmesan cheese

Melt butter in a large skillet, then add cooked, hot cauliflower flowers, turning them until they are well coated with butter. Roll flowers in bread crumbs until coated, then serve, topped with cheese. Serves 4.

CELERY

Preparing
Discard leaves and root and cut off any discolored spots. Scrub stalks with a vegetable brush under running water. Cut celery hearts in half and wash thoroughly.

Quick-cook method
Place stalk pieces, slices, strips, or minced pieces in salted, boiling water to cover in a large skillet or saucepan and cook, covered, until just tender. Place celery heart halves in a small amount of boiling, salted water and cook, covered, until tender.

CREAMED CELERY

2 cups celery, thinly sliced
1½ cups boiling water
2 tablespoons butter or margarine
3 tablespoons flour
¼ teaspoon salt
dash pepper
1¼ cups milk

In a large saucepan, cook celery in boiling water until tender; set aside. Melt butter in a small saucepan over low heat and blend in flour; add salt, pepper, and milk, stirring until smooth. Pour milk sauce over celery and liquid and cook over medium heat for 5 minutes, stirring frequently. Serve on buttered toast. Serves 6 to 8.

FRIED CELERY

3 cups celery, thinly sliced
1 small onion, thinly sliced
3 tablespoons butter or margarine
2 tablespoons water
salt and pepper to taste

Place celery, onion, and water in a large skillet and cook, covered, over high heat for 2 minutes. Remove cover, add butter, salt, pepper, and fry, turning frequently, until lightly browned. Serves 4.

CELERY PARMESAN

3 cups celery, sliced thin, cooked, and drained
3 tablespoons butter or margarine
¼ cup grated Parmesan cheese
1 tablespoon seasoned bread crumbs
salt and pepper to taste

Melt butter in a large skillet, then add celery, salt, and pepper, mixing together well. Remove from heat and add cheese and bread crumbs, mixing until well-blended. Serve at once. Serves 4.

SWEET AND SOUR CELERY

2 cups celery, sliced, cooked, and drained
1 teaspoon flour
½ teaspoon cornstarch
1 tablespoon sugar
¼ teaspoon salt
dash pepper
1 tablespoon vinegar
½ cup warm water
1 egg, beaten
3 tablespoons dairy sour cream

Add all ingredients except celery and sour cream in a large saucepan and cook over medium heat, stirring frequently, to a near boil. Remove from heat and fold in celery and sour cream. Serve at once. Serves 4.

CELERY HEARTS

2 celery hearts, halved
1 teaspoon chopped chives
2 tablespoons butter or margarine
dash marjoram
salt and pepper to taste
½ cup warm water

Fry hearts in butter in a large skillet, turning frequently, until browned. Sprinkle with marjoram, salt, and pepper. Add water, reduce heat, cover and simmer until tender. Serves 4.

CELERY ROOT
[CELERIAC]

Preparing
Cut away tops and stringy root parts and discard. Scrub surface with vegetable brush under running water.

Quick-cook method
Cook whole roots in a large saucepan in boiling, salted water, covered, until tender, at least 35 minutes; drain and peel. If cooking pieces, do not peel roots until just before cooking, as they discolor quickly. Peel roots and slice or dice and drop into boiling, salted water to cover and cook, covered, until tender.

CREAMED CELERY ROOT

3 cups celery root, peeled, diced, cooked, and drained
2 tablespoons butter or margarine
1 cup whipping cream
salt and pepper to taste

Melt butter in a large saucepan, then add whipping cream, salt, and pepper, blending well until smooth. Add celery root and cook over medium heat for 5 minutes, stirring frequently. Serve at once. Serves 4.

CELERIAC SMASH

3 large celery roots, cooked, drained, and peeled
3 tablespoons butter or margarine
1 tablespoon water
½ cup warm milk
salt and pepper to taste

Cut cooked and peeled celery root into chunks and combine with remainder of ingredients in a large bowl. Mash roots, then blend thoroughly with other ingredients. Serve topped with butter. Serves 4.

PAN-FRIED CELERY ROOT

3 cups celery root, peeled and sliced thinly
5 tablespoons butter or margarine
2 tablespoons water
salt and pepper to taste
dash cayenne pepper
paprika

Cook celery in water and 2 tablespoons butter in a large, covered skillet over medium heat until just tender. Add remainder of butter, salt, pepper, and cayenne; raise heat to high and cook, turning frequently until lightly browned. Sprinkle with paprika and serve at once. Serves 4.

CORN

Preparing
Remove the husk and silk at time of cooking, using a vegetable brush to remove the silk. Do not wash.

Quick-cook method
Cook corn on the cob in a large pot of boiling, salted water to cover, covered, for 3 to 5 minutes. For cooked corn, cook the same as for corn on the cob, then remove the kernels with a sharp knife.

SCALLOPED CORN

2 cups corn kernels, cooked
¼ cup milk
¼ cup water
3 tablespoons heavy cream
1 teaspoon sugar
1 teaspoon salt

¼ teaspoon pepper
1 cup unseasoned bread crumbs
2 tablespoons butter or margarine

Mix all ingredients except bread crumbs and butter together in a large bowl. Melt the butter in a small saucepan and mix in the bread crumbs thoroughly. Cover the bottom of a shallow baking dish with half of the butter-crumb mixture, add the corn mixture, then top with the remainder of butter-crumb mixture. Bake at 325°F for 25 minutes. Serves 4.

CORN FRITTERS

1 cup grated corn kernels, cooked 3 minutes in boiling, salted
    water and drained
2 egg yolks, beaten
½ teaspoon salt
dash pepper
1 teaspoon sugar
1 cup Bisquick
1½ teaspoons baking powder
2 egg whites, beaten lightly
shortening

Mix all ingredients except egg whites in a large mixing bowl thoroughly; fold in egg whites last. Form into fritters ½-inch thick and 3 inches in diameter. In a large skillet, fry fritters in hot (375°F) shortening until deep brown on both sides. Drain on absorbent paper and serve with syrup. Makes about 1½ dozen fritters.

CURRIED CORN

1½ cupa corn kernels
1 teaspoon chopped chives
3 tablespoons green pepper, minced
3 tablespoons butter or margarine
¼ teaspoon salt
dash pepper
½ teaspoon curry powder
1 tablespoon warm water
½ cup dairy sour cream

In a large skillet, melt butter over medium heat and cook green pepper until tender, about 1 minute. Add the rest of the ingredients except the sour cream and mix thoroughly. Simmer, covered, for 10 minutes or until corn is tender. Blend in sour cream, raise heat to medium-high, and cook for 5 minutes, stirring constantly. Serve at once. Serves 4.

CREAMED CORN

3 cups corn kernels, cooked
3 tablespoons butter or margarine
1 tablespoon flour
½ teaspoon cornstarch
1⅓ cups light cream
2 tablespoons sugar

Melt butter in a large saucepan, then blend in flour and cornstarch until smooth. Add cream and sugar, stir until smooth, then raise heat to medium and add corn, cooking for 5 minutes. Serves 4.

STOVE-TOP CORN

2½ cups corn kernels
1 small onion, minced
1 teaspoon chopped chives
3 tablespoons butter or margarine
1 tablespoon water
salt and pepper to taste

Combine all ingredients at once in a large skillet, stir a few times, and simmer, covered, for 10 minutes. Remove cover, raise heat to high, and cook until kernels begin to brown, turning frequently. Serve at once. Serves 4.

BAKED CORN

1½ cups corn kernels, cooked
3 tablespoons butter or margarine
4 tablespoons flour
½ cup warm milk
½ teaspoon salt
pepper to taste
3 eggs, beaten well

Melt butter in a large saucepan, then blend in flour until smooth. Add remainder of ingredients except corn, mix well, raise heat to medium, and cook for 3 minutes, stirring frequently. Remove from heat and stir in corn. Pour mixture into a buttered, deep baking dish and bake at 350°F for 25 minutes or until set and lightly browned. Serves 4.

CUCUMBER

Preparing
Cut off ends of cucumbers. If using unpeeled, rinse under running water.

Quick-cook method
Cooked cucumbers must first be peeled. Cut into thick slices or quarter and cook in a large saucepan with salted, boiling water to cover until tender.

CREAMED CUCUMBERS

3 cups cucumbers, peeled, sliced, cooked, and drained
1 tablespoon butter or margarine
¾ cup whipping cream
¼ teaspoon salt

Melt butter in a large saucepan, then blend in salt and whipping cream until smooth. Raise heat to medium, add cucumbers, and cook for 5 minutes, turning frequently. Serve at once. Serves 4.

FRIED CUCUMBERS

3 cups cucumbers, peeled and thinly sliced
1 tablespoon chopped chives or scallion tops
2 tablespoons butter or margarine
1 tablespoon warm butter
½ teaspoon sugar
½ teaspoon salt
¼ teaspoon pepper

Combine all ingredients at once in a large skillet, blend well, then cook, covered, over medium heat for 5 minutes. Remove cover, raise heat, and cook, turning frequently, until cucumbers begin to turn a light brown. Serves 4.

DILLY CUCUMBER STICKS

3 large cucumbers, peeled and cut into sticks
2 tablespoons cold water
½ cup vinegar
1 tablespoon salt
1 tablespoon sugar
½ teaspoon pepper
1 teaspoon dill weed

Mix all marinade ingredients together thoroughly, then pour over cucumber sticks. Cover and refrigerate for at least 3 hours. Drain before serving. Serves 6.

BRAISED CUCUMBERS
3 medium cucumbers, peeled, cut into 1-inch slices
1 large onion, sliced thinly
¼ cup butter or margarine
1 tablespoon sugar
½ teaspoon salt
1 teaspoon lemon juice
¼ cup water
¼ teaspoon dill weed
¾ cup dairy sour cream

In a large saucepan, blend sugar and salt with melted butter; cook over low heat until browned slightly. Raise heat to medium, then add cucumbers and onion, stirring constantly, until the onions are tender. Add water, dill weed, and lemon juice. Cook covered for 6 minutes. Stir in sour cream, mix well, and serve. Serves 4 to 6.

EGGPLANT

Preparing
Trim the stem cap from the eggplant and rinse.

Quick-cook method
Cut eggplant into thick slices (about ¾-inch) and place in a large skillet with a small amount of water. Cook covered over medium heat, turning once, until just tender. Slices can be peeled easily, if necessary, after cooking.

FRIED EGGPLANT
1 large eggplant, pared and sliced thinly
½ cup flour
2 eggs, beaten well
⅔ cup seasoned bread crumbs
olive or vegetable oil

Dip eggplant slices in flour, then egg, and then in bread crumbs. Fry slices in a large skillet in hot oil (375°F) until tender and lightly browned. Serves 4 to 6.

GRILLED EGGPLANT

1 large eggplant, cut into ¾- to 1-inch slices
¼ cup olive oil
⅛ teaspoon salt
dash pepper

Mix salt and pepper with olive oil, then brush both sides of the eggplant slices with oil. Place slices on a baking sheet and cook about 5 inches from broiler, turning once. Slices are done when tender and browned on both sides. Serves 4.

STUFFED EGGPLANT

1 large eggplant
3 tablespoons butter or margarine
3 tablespoons onion, minced
3 tablespoons seasoned bread crumbs
1 egg yolk, beaten
salt and pepper to taste

In a large saucepan, boil eggplant in salted water to cover until just tender; drain and let cool a few minutes. Scrape out inside of eggplant, being careful not to break the skin, and set aside. Melt butter in a large saucepan, then add onion, eggplant pulp, bread crumbs, egg yolk, and salt and pepper, blending all thoroughly. Use mixture to refill shell. Place eggplant on a baking sheet and bake at 375°F until top is browned, at least 20 minutes. Serves 4.

EGGPLANT PARMESAN

1 large eggpant, cut into ½-inch slices
½ cup olive oil or vegetable oil
¾ cup seasoned bread crumbs
3 eggs, beaten well
⅔ cup grated Parmesan cheese

Dip eggplant slices first in egg, then in bread crumbs, coating thoroughly. Fry in hot oil in a large skillet until browned on both sides. Layer browned eggplant slices in a shallow baking dish, sprinkle with cheese, and bake at 325°F for 25 minutes or until cheese is browned. Serves 4.

ELEGANT EGGPLANT SOUFFLÉ

1 medium eggplant, peeled, cubed, cooked, drained, and mashed
1 tablespoon onion, grated
3 tablespoons butter or margarine
2 tablespoons flour
1 cup milk
½ cup grated mild Cheddar cheese
¾ cup unseasoned bread crumbs
1 teaspoon salt
¼ teaspoon pepper
2 egg yolks, beaten
2 egg whites, beaten stiffly

Melt butter in a large saucepan and blend in flour; add milk and blend thoroughly. Add mashed eggplant, cheese, bread crumbs, onion, salt, pepper, and, last, egg yolks; blend all thoroughly. Fold in egg whites and turn mixture into a buttered, deep baking dish. Place in a pan of hot water and bake at 375°F for 40 minutes, or until set and browned. Serve at once. Serves 4 to 6.

FENNEL

Preparing
Cut away and discard the outer stalks of the bulb portion; trim the rough parts from the fennel tops and discard. Rinse thoroughly.

Quick-cook method
Place the bulb parts (halved, quartered, sliced, or diced) in a small amount of salted, boiling water in a large saucepan and cook, covered, until tender.

BAKED FENNEL

2 fennel bulbs, halved, cooked, and drained
1 tablespoon fennel leaves, chopped
2 tablespoons melted butter or margarine
1 tablespoon grated Gouda or Parmesan cheese

Arrange fennel halves, cut side up, in a shallow baking dish. Drizzle melted butter over halves, then sprinkle with leaves and cheese. Bake at 350°F for 10 minutes. Serves 4.

FENNEL FRY

2 large fennel bulbs, sliced thinly
1 tablespoon onion, minced
2 tablespoons water
2 tablespoons butter or margarine
salt and pepper to taste

In a large skillet, cook fennel, onion, water, and butter over medium heat, covered, for 5 minutes. Remove cover, sprinkle with salt and pepper, raise heat to high, and cook, turning frequently, until fennel slices begin to brown. Serves 4.

FENNEL MARINADE

3 large fennel bulbs, cooked, drained, and diced
⅔ cup vegetable oil
½ cup lemon juice
1 tablespoon white vinegar
1 small bay leaf, crushed
1 teaspoon salt
1 teaspoon sugar
½ teaspoon pepper

Combine marinade ingredients in a large saucepan, bring to a boil, and drop in diced fennel. Remove from heat and allow to cool. Refrigerate overnight. Drain before serving. Serves 6.

GREENS: SWISS CHARD, KALE, LETTUCE, SPINACH, BEET GREENS, AND TURNIP TOPS

Preparing
Cut off any roots and discard; discard any yellow or wilted leaves. Rinse lettuce and leafy greens in running water, then drain well. For other greens,

swish them around in a large pot of cold water several times, lifting each time, then drain. After washing beet tops and turnip tops, strip leaves and discard stems.

Quick-cook method
Place greens in a large saucepan with a very small amount of water and salt, cover, and cook over medium heat until tender, turning a few times while cooking. **Note:** the "ribs" of Swiss chard should be cooked in water to cover a few minutes, covered, before adding chard leaves.

PUNGENT MUSTARD GREENS
1 pound mustard greens, cooked, drained, and chopped
1 small onion, minced
3 tablespoons butter or margarine
salt and pepper to taste
dash marjoram

Melt butter in a large skillet and cook onion over low heat until tender. Add greens, sprinkle with salt, pepper, and marjoram, mix well, raise heat to high, and cook another 3 minutes, turning frequently. Serves 4.

CREAMED BEET GREENS
1 pound beet tops, cooked, drained, and chopped
1 tablespoon butter or margarine
½ teaspoon flour
1 tablespoon milk
½ cup half-and-half
1 tablespoon vinegar

Melt butter in a large saucepan, then blend in flour and milk until smooth; add half-and-half and vinegar, blending until smooth. Raise heat to medium, add beet tops, and cook for 3 minutes, stirring frequently. Serves 4.

FAST FRIED SPINACH
1½ pounds spinach, finely chopped
1 scallion, minced
2 tablespoons butter or margarine
½ teaspoon lemon juice
salt and pepper to taste

Combine all ingredients at once in a large skillet, mix well, and cook, covered, over medium heat for 3 minutes. Remove cover, raise heat to high, and cook, turning constantly, for another 3 minutes. Serves 4.

CHILLED SPINACH RING

2 cups spinach, chopped finely
½ teaspoon chopped chives
1 envelope unflavored gelatine
1 cup cold water
½ teaspoon salt
½ teaspoon dry mustard
¼ teaspoon pepper
¼ cup lemon juice
3 hard-cooked eggs, chopped
⅔ cup cottage cheese

Sprinkle gelatine over cold water in a large saucepan and stir, over low heat, until dissolved. Remove from heat and stir in remainder of ingredients except spinach. Let stand. When mixture begins to gel, fold in spinach, then turn mixture into a large ring mold and chill for at least 4 hours. Serves 6.

SUCCULENT SWISS CHARD

1 pound Swiss chard ribs, cut into 2-inch pieces (save the leaves
    to cook as greens)
1 teaspoon onion, minced
1 tablespoon water
¼ pound butter or margarine
salt and pepper to taste
dash marjoram

Cook ribs and onions in water in a large skillet over medium heat, covered, until ribs are tender. Remove cover, add butter, salt, pepper, and marjoram; cook another 3 minutes. Lift ribs out of the butter, then retain butter-onion sauce to drizzle over ribs. Serves 4.

CHEDDARED SWISS CHARD

1 pound Swiss chard, the ribs cut into 1-inch pieces and the leaves
    cooked and drained
1 tablespoon butter or margarine
1 tablespoon flour
¼ cup milk
½ teaspoon salt
½ cup grated Cheddar cheese

Melt butter in a large saucepan, then blend in flour; add milk and salt, blending until smooth. Add cheese and blend until smooth. Add cooked chard, mix well, then turn mixture into a buttered, shallow baking dish and bake at 325°F for 20 minutes. Serves 4.

CREAMED KALE

1 pound kale, cooked and drained
1 tablespoon butter or margarine
1 tablespoon flour
2/3 cup milk
salt and pepper to taste

Melt butter in a large saucepan, then blend in flour; add milk, salt, and pepper, blending until smooth. Add kale, raise heat to medium, and cook 5 minutes, turning frequently. Serves 4.

JERUSALEM ARTICHOKE

Preparing
Cut any stringy root parts away and discard. Scrub well with a stiff brush under running water or peel— do not peel, however, until just before cooking.

Quick-cook method
Cook Jerusalem artichokes whole or in large chunks, sliced, or diced, in a small amount of salted, boiling water, covered, in a large saucepan, until tender. Unpeeled, whole, cooked artichokes can be peeled easily after allowing to cool.

JERUSALEM ARTICHOKES OREGANO

1¼ pounds Jerusalem artichokes, peeled and sliced thinly
2 tablespoons water
¼ pound butter or margarine
salt and pepper to taste
1 tablespoon vegetable oil
1 teaspoon dried oregano

Cook the artichokes with the water, butter, salt and pepper in a large, covered skillet for 2 minutes over high heat. Remove cover, add oil, and continue cooking, turning frequently, until lightly browned. Top with sprinkled oregano. Serves 4.

CREAMED JERUSALEM ARTICHOKES

2 pounds Jerusalem artichokes, cooked, drained, peeled and sliced
2 tablespoons butter or margarine
1 tablespoon flour
2/3 cup evaporated milk
salt and pepper to taste
paprika

Melt butter in a large saucepan, then blend in flour; add milk and salt and pepper, blending until smooth. Add artichoke slices, raise heat to medium, and cook for 5 minutes, turning frequently. Sprinkle with paprika and serve. Serves 4 to 6.

KOHLRABI

Preparing
Peel the outer skin and discard. Cut away all but the tender leaves and discard the rest. Rinse once.

Quick-cook method
Cook kohlrabi pieces (slices, chunks, or cubes) in a small amount of salted, boiling water in a large, covered saucepan until tender.

ROBBIE'S CREAMED KOHLRABI
1½ pounds kohlrabi, peeled, sliced, cooked, and drained
3 tablespoons butter or margarine
1 tablespoon flour
½ teaspoon cornstarch
⅔ cup evaporated milk
½ teaspoon salt
pepper to taste

Melt butter in a large saucepan, then blend in flour and cornstarch. Add milk, salt, and pepper; cook over medium heat for 1 minute, stirring constantly. Add sliced kohlrabi and continue cooking 3 minutes, turning frequently. Serves 4.

THE KING'S KOHLRABI
1½ pounds kohlrabi, peeled and sliced thinly
1 cup kohlrabi leaves, chopped
1¾ cups boiling water
1 chicken bouillon cube
salt and pepper to taste
1 teaspoon chopped chives
½ teaspoon basil leaves

Dissolve bouillon cube in boiling water. Add kohlrabi slices and cook in a large saucepan, covered, until tender. Remove cover, lower heat to medium, stir in leaves, salt, and pepper, and cook another 3 minutes. Serves 4.

KOHLRABI CHOP-CHOP

1½ pounds kohlrabi, peeled and chopped
2 tablespoons scallion tops, chopped
2 tablespoons water
3 tablespoons butter or margarine
salt and pepper to taste

Cook kohlrabi and scallions in water in a large, covered skillet over high heat for 3 minutes, turning occasionally. Remove cover, add butter, salt, and pepper; mix all well. Continue cooking for 4 minutes, turning frequently. Serves 4.

OKRA

Preparing
Cut off and discard stem ends of pods. Rinse quickly.

Quick-cook method
Slice pods into ½-inch thick slices, drop into a large saucepan with salted, boiling water to just cover. Cook until just tender. Drain at once.

OKLAHOMA FRIED OKRA

4 cups okra, sliced thinly
1 small onion, minced
2 tablespoons water
3 tablespoons butter or margarine
1 teaspoon parsley, chopped
salt and pepper to taste
⅛ teaspoon marjoram

Cook the okra and onion with the water in a large, covered skillet over high heat for 3 minutes. Remove cover, add butter, parsley, salt, pepper, and marjoram, stir well, then cook another 3 minutes, turning frequently. Serves 4 to 6.

SOUTHERN STEWED OKRA

3½ cups okra, sliced
1 large onion, chopped
¼ cup water
1 tablespoon vegetable oil
1 tablespoon lemon juice
salt and pepper to taste

Combine all ingredients at once in a large saucepan, mix well, then cover and simmer until onions are tender. Serve at once. Serves 4 to 6.

ONIONS AND LEEKS

Preparing
For scallions and leeks, cut away and discard roots; trim discolored tops and discard; peel outer layer of skin and discard; rinse well. For bulb onions, trim any root parts and stem and discard; peel away only the outermost layer of skin and discard; do not wash.

Quick-cook method
Cook scallions (green onions) and leeks whole in a covered skillet in enough salted, boiling water to cover until tender. Cook bulb onions whole in a large saucepan in enough salted, boiling water to cover until tender.

CREAMED ONIONS
5 medium onions
2 tablespoons butter or margarine
2 tablespoons flour
1 cup milk
½ teaspoon salt
⅛ teaspoon pepper

In a large saucepan, cook onions in boiling water to cover until tender; drain; chop onions coarsely and set aside. Melt butter in a large saucepan and blend in flour until smooth; add milk, salt, and pepper and cook, over medium heat, stirring constantly until smooth. Add chopped onions and blend. Serve at once. Serves 4.

GLOUCESTER ONIONS
1 dozen small onions
2 tablespoons water
5 tablespoons butter or margarine
2 tablespoons sugar
1 tablespoon brown sugar

Cook onions in water in a small, covered skillet over medium heat for 3 minutes. Remove cover, add butter, sugar, and brown sugar, stirring well, and continue cooking, turning often, until onions are tender and well-glazed. Serves 4.

OLD-FASHIONED ONION RINGS

3 large onions, sliced into ⅓-inch slices
milk to cover
1 cup flour
2 cups water
1 egg white, beaten
¼ teaspoon salt
2 tablespoons vegetable oil
shortening

Place onion slices in a shallow baking dish and pour on just enough milk to cover; cover and let stand 1 hour; drain thoroughly. Make a batter out of flour, egg white, salt, and oil, blending in water last. Push centers out of onion slices, making smaller rings. Dip each ring in batter and fry in hot (375°F) shortening in a large skillet until a medium brown. Drain on absorbent paper. Serves 4 to 6.

CHEESE-STUFFED ONIONS

4 large onions
1 teaspoon flour
1 tablespoon butter or margarine
½ cup seasoned bread crumbs
¼ cup grated Parmesan cheese
salt and pepper to taste

In a large saucepan, boil onions in water to cover for 10 minutes; drain and cool; remove center sections of onions, leaving the outside shell thick enough to hold its shape. Chop onion centers finely and set aside. In a small saucepan, melt butter and blend in flour; add cheese and stir until blended thoroughly, then add bread crumbs, chopped onion, salt, and pepper and mix. Cool mixture a few minutes, then stuff onions. Place onions in a shallow baking dish and bake at 325°F for 25 minutes. Serves 4.

THURSDAY-NIGHT BAKE

1 dozen small onions
3 tablespoons butter or margarine
2 tablespoons flour
⅓ cup milk
1⅓ cups creamed cottage cheese
salt and pepper to taste

In a large saucepan, cook onions in salted boiling water to cover for 5 minutes; drain and place in a buttered, shallow baking dish. In a large saucepan, melt butter and blend in flour until smooth. Over medium heat and stirring constantly, add milk, cottage cheese, salt, and pepper, and cook 3 minutes. Spread mixture over onions and bake at 350°F for 25 minutes, or until top is browned. Serves 4.

ONIONS PARMESAN

4 large onions, sliced
1 medium onion, minced
3 tablespoons melted butter or margarine
1 tablespoon flour
2 tablespoons milk
1 teaspoon salt
¼ teaspoon pepper
½ cup bread crumbs
⅓ cup grated Parmesan cheese

In a large saucepan, mix butter and flour until well-blended; add onion, milk, salt, pepper, bread crumbs, and cheese, and mix all well. Place the onion slices on the bottom of a buttered, deep baking dish, then spread cheese mixture over them. Bake at 300°F for 35 minutes or until onions are tender. Serves 4.

MISTRESS QUICKLY'S FRIED LEEKS

4 medium leeks, sliced thinly
1 tablespoon green pepper, minced
3 tablespoons butter or margarine
salt and pepper to taste

Melt butter in a small skillet, then add leeks, green pepper, salt, and pepper and cook, covered, over low heat until just tender. Remove cover, raise heat to high, and cook another 3 minutes, turning frequently. Serves 4.

PARSNIPS

Preparing
Cut off and discard tops and root ends of mature parsnips, then pare. Do not wash.

Quick-cook method
Cut parsnips into uniform chunks, slices or cubes, then drop into salted, boiling water in a large saucepan and cook, covered, until tender. Do not overcook. Drain at once.

FRENCH PARSON'S PARSNIPS

2 cups parsnips, sliced thinly
⅔ cup boiling water
2 tablespoons butter or margarine
¼ teaspoon salt
2 tablespoons sugar

Combine parsnips, water, butter, salt, and 1 tablespoon of sugar in a large saucepan and cook over high heat, stirring frequently, until water evaporates. Sprinkle with 1 tablespoon of sugar, stir a few times, and serve at once. Serves 4.

HONEY-GLAZED PARSNIPS

2 cups parsnips, sliced, cooked, and drained
1 tablespoon water
3 tablespoons butter or margarine
½ teaspoon lemon juice
1 tablespoon brown sugar
2 tablespoons honey

Combine all ingredients at once in a large skillet and cook, over medium heat, until slices are well-glazed and lightly browned. Serves 4.

"SALTED AND BATTERED" PARSNIPS

2 cups parsnips, sliced, cooked, and drained
⅔ cup flour
3 tablespoons flour
1 egg, beaten
¼ teaspoon baking power
¼ teaspoon salt
shortening
brown or powdered sugar

Dip slices into flour and coat well. Make a batter of 3 tablespoons of flour and remaining ingredients. Dip floured slices into batter and coat well, then fry in hot (375°F) shortening in a large skillet until browned on both sides. Drain on absorbent paper and serve plain or sprinkled with brown or powdered sugar. Serves 4.

PEAS

Preparing
Shell peas from pods and rinse well in cold water.

Quick-cook method
Drop peas into either a skillet or a saucepan in just enough salted, boiling water to cover. Reduce heat to simmer, cover, and cook until tender, about 5 to 7 minutes; drain.

CREAMED PEAS

3 cups peas, cooked and drained
2 tablespoons butter or margarine
1 tablespoon flour
1 teaspoon sugar
salt and pepper to taste
½ cup dairy sour cream

Melt butter in a large skillet, then blend in flour; add sugar, salt, and pepper, then blend. Add peas, mixing well, then raise heat to medium. Fold in sour cream and cook 3 minutes, stirring frequently. Serves 6.

LEMONY PEAS

2 cups peas, cooked and drained
¼ cup butter or margarine
1 tablespoon lemon juice
½ teaspoon grated lemon peel

Melt butter in a large saucepan, then blend in lemon juice and peel. Add hot peas, mix well, and serve at once. Serves 4.

DILLED PEAS

2 cups peas, cooked and drained
3 tablespoons butter or margarine
¼ teaspoon lemon juice
1 tablespoon dill, minced

Melt butter in a large saucepan, blend in lemon juice, then stir in dill; cover and simmer for 5 minutes. Remove cover, stir in hot peas, and serve at once. Serves 4.

GREEN PEPPERS

Preparing
Rinse pepper shells in cold water. Halve peppers, cut away stems and pith, then rinse to remove any remaining seeds. For stuffed peppers: slice off stem and part of top, then rinse out seeds.

Quick-cook method
For whole peppers that are to be stuffed: drop seeded peppers into a large saucepan in which is a large quantity of salted, boiling water; boil for 4 to 5 minutes, then remove and rinse in cold water. For slices, rings, or strips: drop pieces into a large saucepan in which is just enough salted, boiling water to cover; cover and cook for 3 minutes, then drain.

PETER PIPER'S SCALLOPED PEPPERS

5 large green peppers, diced, cooked, and drained
½ cup unseasoned bread crumbs
⅓ cup grated Cheddar cheese
½ cup milk
salt and pepper to taste
2 tablespoons butter or margarine

Place a layer of diced peppers on the bottom of a buttered, shallow baking dish; sprinkle with bread crumbs, then cheese. Continue until peppers, bread crumbs, and cheese are used. Pour milk over all, then sprinkle with salt and pepper and dot top with pieces of butter. Bake at 375°F for 20 minutes or until top is well browned. Serves 4 to 6.

VEGETARIAN STUFFED PEPPERS

4 large green peppers, cooked and drained
2 cups cooked rice (brown rice preferred)
1 tablespoon chopped chives
1 cup carrots, grated
2 tablespoons melted butter or margarine
1 teaspoon salt
½ teaspoon pepper
dash marjoram

Combine stuffing mixture ingredients and mix well. Use mixture to stuff pepper shells, then place shells in a lightly buttered deep baking dish and bake, covered, at 300°F for 15 minutes. Remove cover, raise heat to 350°F, and bake another 10 minutes. Serves 4.

CALIFORNIA CREAMED PEPPERS
4 large green peppers, diced, cooked, and drained
2 tablespoons butter or margarine
1 tablespoon flour
½ cup half-and-half
salt and pepper to taste

Melt butter in a large saucepan, then blend in flour until smooth. Add peppers, half-and-half, salt, and pepper, blending well. Cover and simmer for 5 minutes. Stir once before serving. Serves 4.

FRISCO FRIED PEPPERS
5 large green peppers, sliced thinly
1 scallion, sliced thinly
2 tablespoons water
2 tablespoons olive oil
½ teaspoon dried oregano
1 teaspoon parsley flakes
garlic salt to taste
pepper to taste

Combine peppers, scallion, and water in a large skillet and cook, over high heat, until water boils off. Add olive oil, reduce heat to medium-high, and cook until peppers just begin to brown. Remove from heat, add oregano, parsley, garlic salt, and pepper, stir well, and serve at once. Serves 4.

POTATOES

Preparing
Wash potatoes in cold water, using a gentle brush to remove grit if necessary. Pare or leave unpared, depending on the cooking method described below.

Quick-cook method
Cook whole, unpared potatoes in a large, covered saucepan in about 1½ inches of salted, boiling water until tender (30 to 40 minutes). Pare and cook quarters, slices, or cubes in 1 inch of salted, boiling water, covered, until tender (15 to 20 minutes). **Note:** do not boil potatoes too vigorously. Pare whole, cooked potatoes when cool enough to handle.

To bake potatoes: pat whole potatoes dry after washing, then rub skins with butter or margarine. Pierce potatoes with a fork evenly. Bake potatoes on the oven rack at 425°F until tender (35 to 45 minutes).

HEAVENLY HASHED POTATOES

3 large potatoes, cooked, drained, pared, and chopped
salt and pepper to taste
2 tablespoons flour
¼ pound butter or margarine

In a large bowl, sprinkle potatoes with salt, pepper, and flour; toss a few times. Melt butter in a large skillet, then cook the potatoes over medium-high heat, turning frequently, until well-browned. Serves 4.

POTATO PANCAKES

3 large potatoes, pared and sliced
1 small onion, sliced
2 eggs
1 teaspoon salt
dash pepper
vegetable oil

Place eggs in a blender, then turn to a high speed. Begin dropping potato slices into blender, adding a slice of onion frequently. Add salt and pepper last, and continue blending for 1 minute. Heat oil at medium-high heat (350°F) in a large skillet or on a griddle, then place 2 tablespoons of mixture in a circle for each pancake. Brown on both sides. Makes about 3 dozen pancakes.

FANCY POTATOES EN CASSEROLE

4 medium potatoes, pared and sliced thinly
1 large onion, sliced thinly
¼ cup butter or margarine
2 tablespoons flour
1 cup milk
1 cup grated Cheddar cheese
½ teaspoon Worcestershire sauce
salt and pepper to taste

Place potatoes on the bottom of buttered, deep baking dish; place onion slices on top. In a large saucepan, melt butter, then blend in flour; over medium heat, add milk, cheese, Worcestershire sauce, salt, and pepper; stir constantly until smooth. Pour cheese sauce over potatoes and onions and bake, covered, at 375°F for 25 minutes. Remove cover, reduce heat to 325°F, and bake another 20 minutes. Serves 4 to 6.

CREAMED SPUDS

4 medium potatoes, pared and sliced
½ teaspoon chopped chives
2 tablespoons melted butter or margarine
1 teaspoon flour
⅓ cup light cream
1 tablespoon grated Parmesan cheese

Place potatoes in a buttered, shallow baking dish. Melt butter in a small saucepan, then blend in flour, stirring until smooth. Add chives, cream, and cheese, raise heat to medium, and cook, stirring constantly, until smooth. Pour mixture over potatoes and bake, covered, at 375°F for 35 minutes, or until potatoes are tender. Serves 4.

TWICE-BAKED POTATOES

4 large potatoes, baked, cut in half lengthwise, with the centers
    scooped out
2 tablespoons butter or margarine
1 tablespoon milk
1 egg, beaten well
¼ teaspoon salt
pepper to taste
¼ cup grated Cheddar cheese

Mix the potato pulp with the rest of the ingredients until thoroughly blended. Use mixture to fill potato shells. Place stuffed halves in a shallow baking dish and bake at 350°F for 20 minutes or until tops are browned. Top with cheese and bake 1 more minute, or until cheese begins to melt. Serves 8.

DUCHESS POTATOES

2 cups hot mashed potatoes
3 tablespoons melted butter or margarine
½ teaspoon salt
pepper to taste
2 egg yolks, beaten well
2 egg whites, beaten

Mix the potatoes, butter, salt, pepper, and egg yolks in a mixing bowl until blended thoroughly. Turn mixture into a buttered, shallow baking dish. Brush top of mixture with egg whites. Bake in a 350°F oven for 20 minutes or until top is well-browned. Serves 4.

LAYERED TATERS

4 large potatoes, pared and sliced lengthwise into 1-inch thick slices
¼ pound melted butter or margarine
¾ cup unseasoned bread crumbs
salt and pepper to taste

Salt and pepper the potato slices, then dip them in melted butter. Next, dip slices into bread crumbs until well coated. Layer potato slices in buttered, shallow baking dish and bake at 400°F for 35 minutes or until slices are tender and browned. Serves 4 to 6.

FLORIDA FRIED SWEET POTATOES

3 large sweet potatoes, pared and chopped
¼ cup water
3 tablespoons butter or margarine
salt and pepper to taste

Combine potatoes and water in a large skillet, and cook, covered, on high for 10 minutes. Remove cover, add butter, salt, and pepper, reduce heat to medium, and cook, turning frequently, until lightly browned. Serves 4 to 6.

QUICK CANDIED SWEETS

4 large sweet potatoes, pared and sliced into ½-inch thick slices
¼ pound butter or margarine
⅛ teaspoon salt
½ cup sugar
1 tablespoon cinnamon
1¾ cups water
1 cup sugar

Melt butter in a large skillet over very low heat and cook potato slices, covered, for 5 minutes. Sprinkle potatoes with salt, ½ cup sugar, and cinnamon, then cover and cook another 5 minutes. Dissolve 1 cup sugar in water and pour over potatoes. Bring to a boil, reduce heat, and simmer until potatoes are tender. Serves 4 to 6.

TRADITIONAL CANDIED SWEET POTATOES

4 large sweet potatoes, cooked, drained, pared, and sliced
3 tablespoons butter or margarine
2 tablespoons water
3 tablespoons brown sugar
3 tablespoons honey
dash salt

Melt butter in a small saucepan, then blend in water, brown sugar, honey, and salt until smooth. Place potato slices in a shallow baking dish, then pour syrup over. Bake, covered, at 300°F for 30 minutes; remove cover and bake another 20 minutes. Serves 4 to 6.

RUTABAGA

Preparing
Cut off stem tops and discard. Wash and pare thin outer layer of skin and discard.

Quick-cook method
Drop whole, quartered, sliced, or diced rutabagas into a large saucepan in which is a large quantity of salted, boiling water and cook, covered, until tender (25 to 35 minutes for whole rutabagas, 5 to 15 minutes for pieces).

CANDIED RUTABAGAS

3 medium rutabagas, pared, diced, cooked, and drained
¾ cup cooking water, retained from rutabagas
5 tablespoons butter or margarine
1 tablespoon sugar
½ teaspoon salt

Melt butter in a large saucepan, then blend in sugar, salt, and water. Add rutabagas, mix well, and simmer, covered, for 10 minutes, shaking the pan frequently. Serves 4 to 6.

ALEXANDER'S RAGTIME RUTABAGAS

3 medium rutabagas, pared, sliced, cooked, and drained
⅓ cup of cooking water, retained from rutabagas
3 tablespoons butter or margarine
1 tablespoon sugar
½ teaspoon salt
½ cup whipping cream

Melt butter in a large saucepan, then blend in sugar, salt, water, and whipping cream. Stir in rutabagas and cook over medium heat for 5 minutes, stirring frequently. Serves 4 to 6.

GOLDEN FRIED RUTABAGAS

3 medium rutabagas, pared, diced, cooked, and drained
3 tablespoons butter or margarine
1 teaspoon brown sugar

Melt butter in a large skillet, then cook rutabagas over medium-high heat until they just begin to brown. Remove from heat, sprinkle with brown sugar, and serve at once. Serves 4 to 6.

POLYNESIAN RUTABAGAS

3 medium rutabagas, pared, diced, cooked, and drained
3 tablespoons butter or margarine
1 tablespoon water
1 tablespoon brown sugar
1 tablespoon honey
¼ teaspoon cinnamon
¼ teaspoon ginger
1 teaspoon salt
½ teaspoon pepper

Melt butter in a large saucepan, then blend in remainder of sauce ingredients, stirring until smooth. Add rutabagas, mix well, and cook, over low heat, stirring frequently, for 10 minutes. Serves 4 to 6.

LEMONY RUTABAGAS

3 large rutabagas, pared, sliced, or diced; cooked and drained
¼ pound butter or margarine
1 tablespoon water
1 tablespoon lemon juice
1 teaspoon grated lemon peel

Melt butter in a large saucepan, then blend in water, lemon juice, and lemon peel. Add rutabagas, stir well, and simmer, covered, for 5 minutes. Serve at once. Serves 4 to 6.

SQUASH
(Summer: Zucchini, Pattypan, Crooked Neck;
Winter: Acorn, Banana, Butternut, Hubbard, Pumpkin)

Preparing
Summer: cut away and discard stem and blossom ends of squash. Scrub with a gentle brush under running water.

Winter: cut larger squash into portion-sized pieces, then scrape away stringy parts and seeds with a spoon. Acorn and butternut squashes can be halved or quartered.

Quick-cook methods
Summer: put whole summer squashes in a large saucepan in enough salted, boiling water to cover and cook until tender. Place squash slices or cubes in enough salted, boiling water to cover and cook, covered, until tender.
Winter: pare the skin from the squash pieces, slice or dice, and place in a large saucepan with just enough salted boiling water to cover and cook until tender. To bake: place pieces in a buttered baking dish, skin sides down, and rub butter or margarine on the flesh side. Bake at 400°F until tender, about 15 minutes.

CREAMED SUMMER SQUASH
2 cups summer squash, diced, cooked, and drained
3 tablespoons butter or margarine
½ teaspoon salt
¼ teaspoon pepper
1 teaspoon flour
¾ cup dairy sour cream

Melt butter in a large saucepan, then blend in salt, pepper, flour, and sour cream, stirring until smooth. Stir in squash; cover, and simmer for 10 minutes. Serve at once. Serves 4.

BATTERED CROOKED-NECK SQUASH
2 medium crooked-neck squash, sliced
2 eggs, beaten
1 teaspoon salt
2 tablespoons water
1⅓ cups unseasoned bread crumbs
vegetable oil

Mix eggs, salt, and water until well-blended, then dip squash slices into mixture, coating well. Dip each slice in bread crumbs until well-coated. Cook in hot oil (375°F) in a large skillet until browned on both sides. Serves 4 to 6.

PATTYPAN AND CHEESE

3 cups pattypan squash, sliced, cooked, and drained
3 tablespoons butter or margarine
2 tablespoons water
1 teaspoon flour
½ teaspoon salt
¼ teaspoon pepper
½ cup grated mild Cheddar cheese

Melt butter in a small saucepan, then blend in water, flour, salt, pepper, and cheese until smooth. Spoon mixture over cooked squash and serve at once. Serves 4 to 6.

STUFFED SQUASH

6 small crooked-neck squash, cooked whole and drained
⅓ cup unseasoned bread crumbs
2 tablespoons onion, grated
salt and pepper to taste

Cut squashes in half lengthwise and scoop out meat with a spoon, leaving only the shells. In a large bowl, mix squash, bread crumbs, onion, salt, and pepper thoroughly. Spoon mixture into the squash shells, place halves on a baking sheet, and bake at 375°F until tops are well browned. Serves 4 to 6.

SQUASH BISCUITS

1 cup summer squash, sliced, cooked, drained, and sieved
1 egg, beaten well
½ cup sugar
1 tablespoon melted butter or margarine
1 cup scalded milk
¼ teaspoon salt
⅓ package dry yeast, dissolved in ¼ cup warm water
1 cup flour

Blend the sieved squash, egg, sugar, butter, and milk thoroughly; let cool. Add dissolved yeast and flour and mix well. Cover and let rise in a warm place overnight. Shape into 2-inch biscuits and let rise 25 minutes. Place on a baking sheet and bake at 375°F for 12 to 15 minutes until lightly browned. Makes about 1½ dozen.

ZACHARY'S ZUCCHINI AND CHEESE
2 medium zucchinis, thinly sliced
3 tablespoons butter or margarine
¼ cup water
¼ cup grated Parmesan cheese
salt and pepper to taste

Melt butter in a large skillet, then add squash and water and cook, covered, for 5 minutes. Remove cover, lower heat to medium, and add cheese, stirring well. Remove from heat and sprinkle with salt and pepper. Serve at once. Serves 4.

ITALIAN ZUCCHINI
2 medium zucchinis, thinly sliced
1 medium tomato, chopped
2 scallions, thinly sliced
¼ teaspoon sugar
salt and pepper to taste
¼ cup water
2 tablespoons olive or vegetable oil

Combine all ingredients at once in a large skillet and mix thoroughly. Simmer, covered, until zucchini slices are tender. Serves 4.

ZESTY BAKED ZUCCHINI
2 medium zucchinis, sliced
½ cup half-and-half
¼ teaspoon salt
⅛ teaspoon pepper
1 teaspoon dill, minced
dash cayenne pepper
2 tablespoons grated Parmesan cheese

Combine half-and-half, salt, pepper, dill, and cayenne in a mixing bowl and mix well. Place zucchini slices on the bottom of a buttered, shallow baking dish, then spread mixture over top; sprinkle cheese over all. Bake, covered, at 300°F for 25 minutes. Remove cover, raise heat to 375°F, and bake another 20 minutes. Serves 4 to 6.

ZUCCHINI FRITI

2 medium zucchinis cut lengthwise into ¼-inch slices
1 cup flour
2 eggs, beaten well
olive oil

Dip slices in flour until well-coated, then in eggs, and then in flour again. Fry in hot olive oil in a large skillet until browned on both sides. Serves 4.

STUFFED ZUCCHINI

2 medium zucchinis
2 tablespoons celery, minced
2 scallions, thinly sliced
1 tablespoon butter or margarine
1 tablespoon flour
½ cup milk
1 cup seasoned bread crumbs
1 teaspoon salt
¼ teaspoon pepper

Cut zucchinis in half lengthwise, scoop out pulp, and set the shells aside. In a small saucepan, boil zucchini pulp in water to cover for 3 minutes; drain. In a large saucepan, melt butter and blend in flour; add milk gradually, stirring constantly, and cook over medium heat until thick and smooth. Add zucchini pulp, celery, scallions, bread crumbs, salt, and pepper and mix thoroughly. Fill the shells with the mixture and place in a shallow baking dish. Bake at 375°F for 25 minutes. Serves 4.

GLAZED SQUASH

4 cups winter squash, pared, diced, cooked and drained
3 tablespoons butter or margarine
½ teaspoon lemon juice
2 tablespoons water
2 tablespoons brown sugar
1 tablespoon honey

Melt butter in a large skillet, then blend in lemon juice, water, brown sugar, and honey. Stir in squash, cover, and simmer for 10 minutes. Remove cover, raise heat to medium, and cook another 5 minutes, turning frequently. Serves 4 to 6.

WISCONSIN-STYLE SQUASH

4 cups winter squash, pared, diced, cooked, and drained
¼ pound butter or margarine
½ teaspoon salt
½ cup whipping cream

Melt butter in a large saucepan, then blend in salt and whipping cream until smooth. Add cooked squash and cook, covered, over medium heat for 5 minutes, shaking the pan frequently. Reduce heat and simmer for 5 minutes. Serve at once. Serves 4 to 6.

WINTER SQUASH GOUDA

4 cups winter squash, pared, diced, cooked, and drained
2 tablespoons onion, minced
2 tablespoons butter or margarine
¼ cup water
1 teaspoon flour
1 teaspoon salt
½ teaspoon pepper
1 egg, beaten
⅔ cup grated Gouda cheese

Melt butter in a large saucepan, then blend in water, flour, salt, pepper, egg, and cheese, blending until smooth; stir in onion. Remove from heat, stir in squash, and mix well. Turn mixture into a buttered, deep baking dish and bake at 300°F for 25 minutes. Serves 4 to 6.

TOMATOES

Preparing
Wash, cut out, and discard stem. If tomatoes are to be peeled, dip them first into boiling water, then dip them immediately into cold water; skins will slip off easily.

Quick-cook method
Cook tomatoes which have been sliced, quartered, or diced in a few teaspoonsful of water in a saucepan over medium heat until thoroughly heated.

MARTHA'S 'MATERS

3 cups tomatoes, peeled and diced
1 tablespoon onion, minced
2 tablespoons butter or margarine
1 tablespoon water
½ tablespoon salt
¼ teaspoon pepper
⅛ teaspoon nutmeg
½ cup whipping cream

Simmer onion in butter in a large saucepan until tender, but do not brown. Blend in water, salt, pepper, and nutmeg, then add tomatoes and mix well; cover and simmer for 10 minutes. Remove cover, fold in whipping cream, raise heat to medium, and cook for 5 minutes, stirring frequently. Serve at once. Serves 4.

BATTERED TOMATOES

4 firm tomatoes, sliced
⅔ cup milk
½ cup flour
½ teaspoon salt
½ teaspoon sugar
¼ teaspoon pepper
2 eggs, beaten well
¾ cup unseasoned bread crumbs
butter or margarine

Coat tomato slices well with milk, then flour, salt, sugar, and pepper mixture, then eggs; and last bread crumbs. Cook the slices in butter in a large skillet over medium-high heat until lightly browned on both sides. Serves 4.

TOMATO BROIL

4 large tomatoes, halved
1 tablespoon olive oil
salt and pepper to taste
½ teaspoon oregano

Rub cut sides of tomatoes with olive oil, then sprinkle with salt, pepper, and oregano. Place on a baking sheet and broil about 5 inches from broiler for 5 minutes. Serves 4.

OL' MISS FRIED TOMATOES

3 cups tomatoes, diced
1 tablespoon onion, minced
1 tablespoon chopped chives
3 tablespoons butter or margarine
salt and pepper to taste

Combine all ingredients at once in a large skillet, mix well, and co
covered, over medium heat for 5 minutes. Remove cover, raise heat to hi
and cook, turning frequently, for 3 minutes. Serves 4.

TENNESSEE BAKED TOMATOES

5 large tomatoes, diced
1 teaspoon chopped chives
1 teaspoon salt
½ teaspoon pepper
⅔ cup dairy sour cream
5 tablespoons mayonnaise
dash marjoram

Mix all ingredients except chives together and turn into a buttered, shall
baking dish. Sprinkle top with chives. Bake, covered, at 350°F for 10 m
utes. Remove cover and bake another 10 minutes. Serves 4 to 6.

TANGY TOMATOES

4 large tomatoes, diced
1 tablespoon onion, minced
3 tablespoons butter or margarine
1 tablespoon water
¼ teaspoon salt
¼ teaspoon pepper
½ teaspoon curry powder
½ teaspoon cinnamon

Melt butter in a large saucepan and cook onion in butter until tender. A
water, salt, pepper, curry powder, and cinnamon, blending all well. A
tomatoes, turning pieces until covered with sauce, and simmer, covered,
10 minutes. Serves 4.

GARDEN STATE TOMATO BAKE

5 large tomatoes, diced
3 tablespoons melted butter or margarine
½ teaspoon salt
½ teaspoon sugar
¼ teaspoon pepper
⅓ cup seasoned bread crumbs

Combine all ingredients at once in a buttered, shallow baking dish and mix well. Bake at 400°F for 15 minutes. Serves 4 to 6.

TEXAS FRIED TOMATOES

6 medium green tomatoes, sliced thinly
1 teaspoon salt
¼ teaspoon pepper
1 cup flour
1 tablespoon vegetable oil
3 tablespoons butter or margarine
2 tablespoons brown sugar

Melt butter in a large skillet and blend with oil. Mix flour with salt and pepper. Dip tomato slices in flour and fry over high heat until tender. Serve hot, sprinkled lightly with brown sugar. Serves 4 to 6.

TURNIPS

Preparing
Trim away and discard stem tops. Pare thin layer of outer skin. Rinse in cold water.

Quick-cook method
Cook turnips whole, quartered, sliced, or diced in salted, boiling water in a large saucepan, covered, until tender (25 to 35 minutes for whole turnips, 5 to 10 minutes for pieces).

TALLY-HO TURNIPS

2 cups turnips, diced, cooked, and drained
2 tablespoons butter or margarine
1 teaspoon sugar
⅓ cup whipping cream

Melt butter in a large skillet, then blend in sugar and whipping cream. Add turnips, mix well, and simmer, covered, for 5 minutes. Remove cover, raise heat to medium, and cook another 5 minutes, turning frequently. Serve at once. Serves 4.

GLAZED TURNIPS

2 cups turnips, diced, cooked, and drained
3 tablespoons butter or margarine
1 tablespoon sugar
1 tablespoon brown sugar

Melt butter in a large skillet, then blend in sugar and brown sugar. Add turnips, raise heat to medium-high, and cook, turning frequently, until well glazed, about 5 minutes. Serves 4.

TURNIPS INDIA

2 cups turnips, sliced, cooked, and drained
1 tablespoon onion, minced
3 tablespoons butter or margarine
½ teaspoon salt
¼ teaspoon pepper
1 teaspoon curry powder
⅔ cup half-and-half

Melt butter in a large saucepan. Add onion and simmer, covered, until tender. Blend in salt, pepper, curry powder, and half-and-half. Add turnips, mix well, and simmer for 10 minutes, stirring occasionally. Serves 4.

CHEDDAR TURNIPS

2 cups turnips, sliced, cooked, and drained
2 tablespoons butter or margarine
1 tablespoon water
1 tablespoon flour
½ teaspoon salt
½ teaspoon sugar
½ teaspoon grated mild Cheddar cheese

Melt butter in a large saucepan, then blend in water, flour, salt, and sugar, blending until smooth. Raise heat to medium and add cheese, stirring until smooth. Remove from heat, add turnips, and blend well. Serve at once. Serves 4.

BEEFED-UP TURNIPS

2 cups turnips, diced, cooked, and drained
2 tablespoons onion, minced
3 tablespoons butter or margarine
1 teaspoon flour
¼ teaspoon pepper
1 beef bouillon cube dissolved in 1 cup water
paprika

Melt butter in a large saucepan, then add onion and simmer until tender. Blend in flour, pepper, and water. Add turnips, mix well, and simmer, covered, for 10 minutes. Sprinkle with paprika and serve. Serves 4.

RHUBARB

Preparing
Cut away leaves of root tips (never use leaves) and discard. Wash stalks under running water to remove grit and dirt, then drain. If stalks are not young and tender, they will need peeling like celery. Peel away the tough, stringy outer part of the stalk and discard.

Quick-cook method
Place 1-inch long rhubarb pieces in a skillet and dot lightly with water (use sparingly when cooking rhubarb). Simmer, covered, until pieces can be pierced easily with a fork. Add sugar (about ⅔ cup for every 16 stalks of rhubarb) and continue to cook until soft, stirring frequently. Serve with butter and cinnamon.

BAKED RHUBARB

2½ cups rhubarb, cut into 1½–2-inch pieces
2 tablespoons water
¾ cup sugar
¼ cup brown sugar
¼ teaspoon ginger

In a large casserole, stir together rhubarb, sugar and brown sugar until thoroughly mixed. Next, add water; stir and mix again. Bake, covered, 45 minutes at 350°F. Remove cover, sprinkle ginger on top, reduce heat to 300°F, baking 15 more minutes. Cool and chill before serving. Serves 4 to 6.

SALADS

The rule to remember for successful salads is simple: pick your ingredients fresh, as close to preparation time as possible. As a gardener, you have a distinct advantage over other salad makers. Your vegetables are only a few steps away from the kitchen, whereas the nongardener must make do with produce that is usually shipped from a considerable distance and has been sitting for some time at the grocer's.

Green salads can be made with any variety or combination of lettuce, cabbage, or greens from the garden. Simply toss them with your favorite bottled or homemade dressing, always starting with the dressing on the bottom of the bowl as the first ingredient. In addition, the salad bowl can be enhanced with many of the other vegetables growing in your garden: carrots, onions, peppers, and certain squashes. In fact, there are very few fresh vegetables that aren't suitable for use in a salad.

With your stock of fresh vegetables, it is difficult for you to go wrong in tossing up a salad with whatever vegetables are ready for harvest. The salads in this section, then, are special salads we've found to be very popular, and ones which aren't about to happen by mixing vegetables you pick at random, no matter how happy those ventures prove to be.

BEETS VINAIGRETTE

3 cups cooked, pared, cubed beets
½ cup water
½ cup cider vinegar
3 tablespoons sugar
salt and pepper to taste

Thoroughly chill the beets, then pour the dressing of blended water, vinegar, sugar, and salt and pepper over the beets. Serves 6.

FESTIVAL SALAD

1½ pounds green beans, cut into 1-inch pieces
2 scallions, sliced thin
salt and pepper to taste
3 tablespoons wine vinegar
½ cup vegetable oil

In salted, boiling water, cook beans until just tender; drain and chill. Toss beans with scallions, salt, pepper, vinegar, and oil; refrigerate until served. Serves 4 to 6.

BLUE-RIBBON SALAD

1 cup green beans, cut in 1-inch pieces
1 tablespooon chopped chives
6 tablespoons Italian dressing
2 cups mustard greens or beet tops, broken into bite-sized pieces
2 hard-cooked eggs, sliced

In boiling, salted water, cook beans until just tender; drain. Mix chives and dressing with beans, then marinate at room temperature for at least one hour. Before serving, toss with greens and eggs. Serves 4.

BEAN AND PEA SALAD

2 cups peas
2 cups yellow (wax) beans cut into 1-inch pieces
1 teaspoon sugar
salt and pepper to taste
½ teaspoon lemon juice
6 tablespoons mayonnaise

In boiling, salted water, cook peas and beans until just tender; drain well. Mix remaining ingredients, then pour over vegetables and toss thoroughly; refrigerate until served. Serves 4 to 6.

HOME-STYLE BEAN AND RADISH SALAD

1½ cups green beans, cut into 1-inch pieces
1 scallion, thinly sliced
6 radishes, thinly sliced
½ teaspoon sugar
2 tablespoons wine vinegar
1 tablespoon water
2 tablespoons vegetable oil

In boiling, salted water, cook beans until just tender; drain well. Toss with scallion and radishes. Blend sugar, vinegar, water, and oil, then toss with vegetables; refrigerate until served. Serves 4 to 6.

BROCCOLI BRAVO
1 large head broccoli, sliced
1 small onion, minced
3 tablespoons mayonnaise
salt and pepper to taste
¼ teaspoon sugar
1 tablespoon sour cream
1 teaspoon white vinegar
1 tablespoon vegetable oil

Discard tougher parts of broccoli stalk, then slice the remainder thinly; drop into boiling, salted water and cook until tender, just a few minutes. Just before draining, drop onion into water, stir, then drain broccoli and onion and chill. Blend mayonnaise, salt, pepper, sugar, sour cream, vinegar, and oil thoroughly, then serve over broccoli. Serves 4 to 6.

CABBAGE CREAM SLAW
½ small cabbage, chopped finely
pepper to taste
¼ teaspoon salt
½ pint sweet cream
3 tablespoons sugar
2 tablespoons vinegar

Sprinkle pepper and salt over chopped cabbage. In a separate bowl, mix cream with sugar until sugar is dissolved, then whip into a stiff froth, gradually adding vinegar. Toss cream mixture over slaw and chill before serving. Serves 4.

HOT COLESLAW
1½ cups tender cabbage, finely chopped
2 tablespoons grated carrot
5 tablespoons mayonnaise
5 tablespoons sour cream
¼ teaspoon sugar
salt to taste
½ teaspoon lemon juice
½ teaspoon mild prepared mustard
1 tablespoon warm water

In a small amount of salted, boiling water, (just enough to cover), cook, covered, the cabbage and carrots until just tender; drain. Blend mayonnaise, sour cream, sugar, salt, lemon juice, mustard, and water well, then mix with cabbage mixture. Serve at once. Serves 4.

CABBAGE CORNUCOPIA

2 cups tender cabbage, chopped
2 tablespoons minced celery
2 tablespoons minced green pepper
1 tablespoon chopped chives
¾ cup green beans, thinly sliced
5 tablespoons vegetable oil
2 tablespoons vinegar
½ teaspoon sugar
salt and pepper to taste

In a large bowl, toss the cabbage, celery, pepper, chives, and green beans, which are uncooked and sliced wafer-thin. Blend oil, vinegar, sugar, salt, and pepper, then pour over vegetables and mix thoroughly. Serves 4.

CARROT SLAW

2 cups tender cabbage, chopped fine
¾ cup grated carrot
3 tablespoons vinegar
2 tablespoons vegetable oil
salt and pepper to taste
¼ teaspoon dry mustard
1 tablespoon sugar

Combine all ingredients at once and toss thoroughly; refrigerate until served. Serves 4 to 6.

WORLD'S FAIR SALAD

2 cups grated carrot
1 small onion, minced
1 cup salad greens, broken into bite-sized pieces
salt and pepper to taste
6 tablespoons vegetable oil
3 tablespoons vinegar
1 teaspoon sugar
⅛ teaspoon dry mustard

Toss carrot, onion, greens, salt, and pepper. Blend oil, vinegar, sugar, and mustard; pour over vegetables, mix thoroughly. Serves 4.

SOUTHERN SOUR CAULIFLOWER

1 medium head cauliflower, thinly sliced
1 tablespoon chopped chives
3 tablespoons mayonnaise
salt and pepper to taste
⅛ teaspoon sugar
1 tablespoon sour cream
1 teaspoon white vinegar
1 tablespoon vegetable oil

Drop cauliflower into boiling, salted water and cook until just tender; drain and chill. Blend chives, mayonnaise, salt, pepper, sugar, sour cream, vinegar, and oil thoroughly, then serve over cauliflower. Serves 4.

SWEET & SOUR CAULIFLOWER

2 cups lettuce, chopped
¾ cup grated cauliflower
1 tablespoon minced green pepper
1 tablespoon sugar
¼ cup vegetable oil
3 tablespoons white vinegar
salt and pepper to taste

Toss lettuce, cauliflower, and pepper lightly. Blend sugar, oil, vinegar, salt, and pepper; pour over salad and toss lightly. Serves 4.

CELERY SLAW

¾ cup celery, sliced thin
¾ cup tender cabbage, chopped
2 tablespoons vinegar
1 tablespoon vegetable oil
salt and pepper to taste
⅛ teaspoon dry mustard
1 teaspoon sugar

Combine all ingredients at once and toss thoroughly; refrigerate until served. Serves 4.

CARNIVAL SALAD

2 cups corn kernels, cooked, drained, and chilled
1 small green pepper, minced
1 tablespoon chopped chives
1 tablespoon sweet pickle, sliced thinly, then chopped
3 tablespoons mayonnaise
1½ tablespoons sour cream
1 teaspoon vinegar
salt and pepper to taste
¼ teaspoon mild prepared mustard
⅛ teaspoon Worcestershire sauce

Mix corn, pepper, chives, and pickle together. Blend mayonnaise, sour cream, vinegar, salt, pepper, mustard, and Worcestershire sauce. Mix vegetables with mayonnaise mixture. Serves 4.

CUCUMBER ASPIC

2 packets unflavored gelatine
½ cup cold water
1 pint boiling water
3 large cucumbers, pared and grated
1 medium onion, peeled and grated
3 tablespoons white vinegar
salt and pepper to taste

Soak the gelatine in the cold water, then dissolve it in 1 pint of boiling water. Mix the cucumbers, onions, vinegar, salt, and pepper. When the gelatine begins to congeal, blend the vegetable mixture with the gelatine, pour into a 2-quart mold, and chill. Serves 6 to 8.

CUCUMBER CRISP

1 large cucumber, pared and thinly sliced
1 tablespoon sugar
salt and pepper to taste
2 tablespoons water
¼ cup white vinegar

Combine dressing ingredients and mix until sugar is dissolved. Pour dressing over cucumbers. Serves 4.

CUCUMBER COOLER

1 large cucumber, pared and thinly sliced
1 small onion, peeled and sliced
2 tablespoons white vinegar
2 tablespoons vegetable oil
salt to taste
⅓ cup sour cream
paprika

Mix cucumber and onion in a bowl; sprinkle with salt. Combine vinegar and oil, then pour over cucumber and onion. Marinate 2 hours; drain thoroughly. Add sour cream to salad, blend well, then chill. Sprinkle with paprika. Serves 4.

SEBASTIAN SALAD

1 medium eggplant, peeled and cubed
1 clove garlic
½ teaspoon salt
3 tablespoons vinegar
3 tablespoons vegetable oil
¼ teaspoon marjoram
¼ teaspoon sweet basil
salt and pepper to taste
3 large tomatoes, sliced
fresh parsley

Cook cubed eggplant in boiling, salted water 5 minutes, or until just tender; drain. In a mixing bowl, mix ½ teaspoon salt with crushed garlic clove, then add vinegar, oil, marjoram, basil, salt, and pepper; add eggplant and mix thoroughly; refrigerate. Serve over sliced tomatoes and garnish with parsley. Serves 4.

GARDENER'S CHEF SALAD

1 head romaine lettuce, or 2 heads buttercrunch, broken into
        bite-sized pieces
1 small cucumber, pared and thinly sliced
3 tablespoons scallions, sliced thin
2 medium tomatoes, quartered
French dressing
2 hard-cooked eggs, chopped

Toss lettuce, cucumber, scallions, and tomatoes. Divide into four portions, sprinkle with French dressing, garnish with eggs. Serves 4.

LETTUCE DEMIMOND

1 large head iceberg lettuce
¼ cup mayonnaise
½ cup grated mild Cheddar
⅛ teaspoon marjoram
1 scallion, sliced thin
¼ cup celery, sliced thin
fresh parsley, chopped
French dressing

At the core end of the lettuce head and using a sharp knife, remove core, cutting a 2-inch circle, and continue cutting and hollowing, straight down, until within approximately 1 inch of the top of the head; enlarge circle slightly. In a bowl, mix the mayonnaise with cheese and marjoram, then stir in the celery, scallion, and parsley. Use the mixture to stuff the lettuce, then chill until ready. Serve, sliced in ½-inch slices, with French dressing. Serves 4 to 6.

BUTTER DRESSING SALAD

1 head iceberg lettuce, broken into bite-sized pieces
1 large tomato, sliced
2 scallions, sliced thin
3 teaspoons lemon juice
salt and pepper to taste
6 tablespoons melted butter

In salad bowl, toss lettuce, tomato, scallions, lemon juice, salt, and pepper. Melt butter until it just starts to become foamy, then pour over salad and toss quickly. Serve immediately. Serves 4.

TWO-BEAN SALAD

1 cup lima beans
1 cup green beans, cut in 1-inch pieces
1 tablespoon chopped chives
salt and pepper to taste
1 tablespoon wine vinegar
3 tablespoons vegetable oil

In boiling, salted water, cook limas and green beans until just tender; drain and chill. Toss chives and salt and pepper with beans. Mix vinegar and vegetable oil, then toss with vegetables. Serves 4.

WILTED LETTUCE

1 head lettuce
3 scallions, sliced thin
1 teaspoon oregano
1 teaspoon chopped parsley
6 bacon slices, chopped
¼ cup bacon fat
¼ cup vinegar
salt and pepper to taste
½ teaspoon dry mustard
⅛ teaspoon garlic salt

In a salad bowl, mix scallions, oregano, parsley, and the lettuce, broken in bite-sized pieces. Fry bacon until crisp, and drain, reserving fat; crumble bacon and add to salad. In bacon pan, mix ¼ cup bacon fat and remainder of ingredients, cooking and stirring to a boil. Pour mixture over salad, toss quickly, and serve immediately. Serves 4.

ONION SALAD

1 medium onion, sliced thin
¼ cup Italian dressing
½ teaspoon mild prepared mustard
salt and pepper to taste
1 cup lettuce, broken in bite-sized pieces
1 small tomato, sliced

Marinate the onion in well-blended mixture of dressing and mustard for at least one hour. Toss onion-dressing with lettuce and tomato. Serves 2.

PICNIC PEA SALAD

1½ cups peas
2 tablespoons sliced celery
1 tablespoon minced green pepper
2 scallions, thinly sliced
1 small cucumber, thinly sliced
salt and pepper to taste
5 tablespoons vegetable oil
2 tablespoons wine vinegar
1 teaspoon sugar

Cook peas in boiling, salted water until just tender; drain and chill. Toss peas with celery, pepper, scallions, cucumber, salt, and pepper. Combine oil, vinegar, and sugar, then toss with vegetables. Serves 4.

GERMAN POTATO SALAD

1 pound potatoes, unpared
1 medium onion, chopped
3 slices bacon
3 tablespoons vinegar
salt and pepper to taste
½ teaspoon sugar

While potatoes are cooking in boiling, salted water, begin frying bacon in skillet. Add onion to bacon and cook until the bacon is crisp and the onions are tender; drain. Mix vinegar, salt, pepper, and sugar, then crumble bacon and add onion to mixture. Pare cooked potatoes, then dice. Toss potatoes with vinegar mixture and serve at once. Serves 4.

SWISS POTATO SALAD

1 pound boiled potatoes
5 tablespoons Italian salad dressing
1½ cups grated Swiss cheese
½ cup diced celery
3 scallions, thinly sliced
2 tablespoons minced parsley
3 hard-cooked eggs
½ cup mayonnaise
¼ teaspoon dry mustard
salt and pepper to taste

Pare and cube warm potatoes; mix lightly with 2 tablespoons Italian dressing; chill. Combine with cheese, celery, scallions, parsley, and chopped eggs. Blend mayonnaise, mustard, and remainder of salad dressing, pour over potatoes and mix. Season with salt and pepper. Serves 4.

ZESTY POTATO SALAD

2½ cups cooked, pared, diced potatoes
3 tablespoons chopped chives
½ cup celery, thinly sliced
2 tablespoons grated radishes (white radishes preferred)
½ cup mayonnaise
1 teaspoon prepared mild mustard
1 teaspoon vinegar
salt and pepper to taste

Mix vegetables together. Blend mayonnaise, mustard, vinegar, salt, and pepper until smooth, then mix thoroughly with vegetables; refrigerate until served. Serves 4.

OLD-FASHIONED POTATO SALAD
4 large potatoes, cooked, pared, and diced
2 scallions, sliced thin
1 small green pepper, chopped
salt and pepper to taste
2 tablespoons vinegar
2 tablespoons vegetable oil
2 tablespoons mayonnaise
⅛ teaspoon sugar

Toss vegetables with salt and pepper. Blend vinegar, oil, mayonnaise, and sugar, then mix with vegetables; chill until served. Serves 4.

RADISH SLAW
3 cups tender cabbage, finely chopped
½ cup grated radishes (white radishes preferred)
1 tablespoon minced celery
3 tablespoons vinegar
2 tablespoons vegetable oil
salt and pepper to taste
¼ teaspoon dry mustard
1 tablespoon sugar

Combine all ingredients at once and toss thoroughly; refrigerate until served. Serves 4 to 6.

QUICK RELISH MOLD
1 large cucumber, unpared and minced
1 small green pepper, minced
3 scallions, thinly sliced
6 radishes, thinly sliced
3 beef bouillon cubes
3 envelopes unflavored gelatine
1 pint boiling water
½ cup vinegar
1 teaspoon salt
1 pint dairy sour cream

Dissolve bouillon cubes and gelatine in boiling water, then add vinegar and salt; chill until partially set. Add sour cream and blend thoroughly, then add vegetables and mix. Pour into 2-quart mold and chill. Serves 8.

TURNOVER TURNIP SALADE

2 pounds turnips, pared, sliced thin
1 tablespoon chopped chives
½ cup minced celery
salt and pepper to taste
½ teaspoon prepared mild mustard
½ cup mayonnaise
2 tablespoons warm water
paprika

In boiling, salted water, cook turnips until just tender; drain and chill. Combine turnips, chives, celery, salt, and pepper and toss together. Blend mustard, mayonnaise, and water until smooth, then mix with vegetables. Sprinkle with paprika. Serves 4 to 6.

GREAT GRANDMA'S SPINACH SALAD

1 pound spinach
3 tablespoons white vinegar
3 teaspoons mild prepared mustard
½ cup salad oil
1 tablespoon chopped chives
1 teaspoon sugar
salt and pepper to taste

Break spinach into bite-sized pieces in a salad bowl. Combine remainder of ingredients in a bottle and shake until blended thoroughly. Toss dressing in salad; add salt and pepper if needed. Serves 6.

CONTINENTAL SPINACH SALAD

1 pound spinach, broken into bite-sized pieces
4 slices bacon, fried, drained, and crumbled
2 hard-cooked eggs, chopped
1 scallion, thinly sliced
salt and pepper to taste
⅛ teaspoon marjoram
5 tablespoons vegetable oil
2 tablespoons vinegar
1 teaspoon sugar

Toss spinach, bacon, eggs, scallion, salt, pepper, and marjoram in salad bowl. Blend oil, vinegar, and sugar, then toss over vegetables. Serves 4 to 6.

TOMATO ASPIC

2 pounds ripe tomatoes, peeled and diced
1 teaspoon dill
1 teaspoon salt
1 small bay leaf
½ clove garlic
1 small onion, sliced
⅓ cup water
2 tablespoons vinegar
2 tablespoons unflavored gelatine
1 teaspoon sugar

In blender, blend first 6 ingredients until puréed; strain. Heat water and vinegar, then mix gelatine into liquid and heat, over low heat, until dissolved. Mix gelatine mixture with purée, add sugar, then pour into 1-quart mold. Chill until firm, unmold, and serve. Serves 4.

'MATERS TOMATERS

1 large tomato
1 envelope unflavored gelatine
1 cup cold water
2 tablespoons vinegar
½ teaspoon sugar
1 small onion, grated
1 small green pepper, grated
3 stalks celery, minced
1 teaspoon parsley
salt to taste

In blender, purée tomato; strain. Soak gelatine in cold water, then add vinegar, sugar, salt, and purée. When mixture begins to gel, stir in remaining ingredients and pour into 1-quart mold; chill. Serves 2 to 4.

TWO BEAN OR NOT TWO BEAN SALAD

½ pound green beans, cut into 1-inch pieces
½ pound yellow (wax) beans, cut into 1-inch pieces
1 large tomato, cubed
1 scallion, thinly sliced
salt and pepper to taste
dash marjoram
⅛ teaspoon crushed basil
3 tablespoons vegetable oil
1 tablespoon white vinegar

In boiling, salted water, cook beans until just tender; drain and chill. In a salad bowl, toss beans, tomato, scallion, salt, pepper, and marjoram. Blend basil, oil, and vinegar, then pour over vegetables and toss lightly. Serves 4.

TOMATO SALAD DIABLO

6 firm, large tomatoes
½ cup Roquefort cheese
1 8-ounce package cream cheese
⅛ teaspoon Tabasco sauce
1 teaspoon chopped chives
1 tablespoon chopped parsley
3 tablespoons mayonnaise
2 teaspoons unflavored gelatine
½ cup cold water

Cut a slice from the stem ends of the tomatoes and, with a small spoon, scoop out the seed and pulp. Mash the Roquefort smoothly, then blend with cream cheese, Tabasco, chives, parsley, and mayonnaise. In a metal cup, mix the gelatine with the water and set in a pan of hot water until dissolved; cool, then mix thoroughly with cheese mixture. Stuff the tomatoes with mixture, then chill. Slice tomatoes and serve on lettuce. Serves 6.

TOMATO SLAW

3 cups tender cabbage, finely chopped
1 firm tomato, diced
½ teaspoon chopped chives
3 tablespoons vinegar
2 tablespoons vegetable oil
salt and pepper to taste
¼ teaspoon dry mustard
1 tablespoon sugar

Combine all ingredients at once and mix thoroughly; refrigerate until served. Serves 4.

WINE VINEGAR SALAD

1 medium onion, peeled and thinly sliced
1 large green pepper, sliced
2 large tomatoes, sliced
½ small cucumber, thinly sliced
salt and pepper to taste
½ cup wine vinegar
½ cup cold water

In a bowl, toss the vegetables with the salt and pepper lightly. Mix vinegar with water, then pour over vegetables; refrigerate, covered, before serving. Serves 4.

ZIPPY ZUCCHINI SALAD

1 medium zucchini, thinly sliced
2 radishes, grated
1 tablespoon chopped chives
salt and pepper to taste
1 tablespoon wine vinegar
2 tablespoons vegetable oil

Lightly toss vegetables with salt and pepper. Mix vinegar and oil, sprinkle over salad, and toss lightly. Serves 4.

ZUCCHINI AND TOMATO SALAD

3 medium zucchinis, thinly sliced
1 large tomato, sliced
1 tablespoon chopped chives
garlic salt and pepper to taste
1 teaspoon oregano
5 tablespoons vegetable oil
2 tablespoons wine vinegar
½ teaspoon sugar

Toss zucchini, tomato, chives, garlic salt, pepper, and oregano in a bowl. Blend oil, vinegar, and sugar, then pour over vegetables. Toss lightly. Serves 6 to 8.

SOUPS
AND
CHOWDERS

Healthful, unforgettable soups and chowders, without meat, can be made from the vegetables you grow. The recipes presented here will cover the range of vegetables from the beginning of the growing season to the end. You can make a soup every day if you want. These dishes can also be stored, covered, in the refrigerator for a day or two.

Some recipes here call for either white or brown stock. The quick recipes which follow should be used in making them.

QUICK WHITE STOCK

6 chicken bouillon cubes
1¼ quarts cold water
¼ teaspoon pepper
1 clove
dash marjoram
1 tablespoon celery, diced
1 tablespoon onion, diced

Combine all ingredients in a large saucepan, bring to a boil, then reduce heat and simmer for 2 hours. Strain through a cheesecloth and cool. May be refrigerated for several days. Makes about 1 quart.

QUICK BROWN STOCK

8 beef bouillon cubes
2 quarts cold water
1 teaspoon pepper
2 cloves
1 large bay leaf
1 sprig parsley
½ teaspoon thyme
2 tablespoons celery, diced
3 tablespoons carrot, diced
3 tablespoons turnip, diced
1 medium onion, sliced

Combine all ingredients in a large saucepan, bring to a boil, and allow to boil for 10 minutes. Reduce heat and simmer for 2 hours. Strain through a cheesecloth and cool. May be refrigerated for several days. Makes about 1½ quarts.

RASPUTIN'S BORSCHT

1 large tomato, peeled
2 cups beets, pared and grated
4 cups water
1 small onion, peeled and chopped
1 tablespoon lemon juice
¼ cup sugar
¼ teaspoon salt
3 eggs, beaten well

Place beets in a large saucepan and then strain tomato through a fine sieve over them. Add water and onion and simmer 30 minutes. Next, add lemon juice, sugar, and salt and boil 30 minutes longer. Add the hot borscht to the eggs a little at a time, stirring thoroughly during each addition. Serve immediately. Serves 4.

RUSSIAN BEET SOUP

2 cups beets, pared, cooked, and sliced
2 cups water
2 tablespoons sugar
salt and pepper to taste
dash cinnamon
3 tablespoons vinegar
4 eggs, beaten slightly
4 tablespoons sour cream

Combine beets, water, sugar, salt, pepper, and cinnamon in a large saucepan, heat to boiling, reduce heat, and simmer for 15 minutes. Add vinegar and heat to boiling. Drop one egg in each bowl and pour hot beet juice over it, mixing thoroughly; then add beet slices to each bowl. Top each serving with 1 tablespoon sour cream. Serves 4.

CABBAGE AND BEET SOUP

1 small head cabbage, finely chopped
2½ cups beets, pared, cooked, and diced
1 small onion, peeled and chopped
2 quarts brown stock
1 teaspoon salt
¼ teaspooon pepper

Combine all ingredients in a large saucepan and bring to a boil; reduce heat and simmer until cabbage and onions are tender. Serves 8 to 10.

CREAM OF ASPARAGUS SOUP

1 pound asparagus
4 cups milk, scalded
2 tablespoons butter or margarine
2 tablespoons flour
1 teaspoon salt
⅛ teaspoon pepper

Cut approximately 2 inches from tops of asparagus stalks, and cook, uncovered, in boiling, salted water until just tender. Remove and set aside, then cook remainder of asparagus until very soft; drain stalk parts thoroughly, rub through a sieve, and mix sieved asparagus with milk. In a saucepan, melt the butter, blend in the flour, salt, and pepper, then add the sieved asparagus mixture gradually and bring to a boil, stirring constantly and cooking for 3 minutes. Add asparagus tips last and serve immediately. Serves 4 to 6.

CREAM OF BEET SOUP

1 cup beets, pared, cooked, and chopped
1 medium onion, peeled and minced
1 tablespoon butter or margarine
1 cup water
½ cup brown stock
1 teaspoon salt
pepper to taste
1 cup evaporated milk, scalded

In a large skillet over low heat, slowly cook onion in melted butter until the onion turns light yellow. Add the water, beets, and stock and simmer until the onions are soft. Next, add salt, pepper, milk, heat to boiling, and serve at once. Serves 4.

CREAM OF CABBAGE SOUP

½ head tender cabbage, chopped
2 cups boiling water
2 tablespoons butter
1 tablespoon onion, minced
2 tablespoons flour
1 teaspoon salt
⅛ teaspoon pepper
dash cayenne
2 cups milk, scalded

In a large saucepan, combine boiling water with cabbage and cook over low heat until cabbage is very soft; press through a coarse sieve and return liquid to pan. Add butter and onion and simmer for 5 minutes; blend in flour, salt, pepper, and cayenne, simmering another 3 minutes; raise heat to medium and add milk gradually, stirring constantly. Serve at once. Serves 4 to 6.

PEASANT SOUP

½ head tender cabbage, chopped coarsely
1½ quarts cold water
1 pint brown stock
2 teaspoons salt
¼ teaspoon pepper
1 bay leaf
2 medium onions, sliced
1 cup celery, chopped
1 cup beet tops or mustard greens, finely chopped
2 tablespoons vegetable oil

Combine water, stock, salt, pepper, and bay leaf in a large saucepan, heat to boiling, and cook for 10 minutes. While water boils, brown, in hot oil, cabbage, onions, celery, and green tops. Add well-browned vegetables to liquid and continue boiling for 5 minutes; reduce heat and simmer 30 minutes. Serves 8 to 10.

THE CAPTAIN'S CARROT SOUP

3½ cups carrots, thinly sliced
2 tablespoons butter or margarine
1 large onion, peeled and chopped
1 tablespoon flour
1 quart brown stock
¾ cup celery, thinly sliced
2 teaspoons salt
½ teaspoon pepper

Melt butter in a large saucepan and brown the onion; blend in flour, then add the stock. Stir while heating until boiling, cook for 3 minutes, then reduce heat. Add remainder of ingredients and simmer for 1 hour. Let cool a few minutes, rub through a coarse sieve, then return to high heat and cook for 5 minutes. Serves 6.

CREAM OF CARROT SOUP

2 cups carrots, chopped
2 cups water
1 medium onion, peeled and sliced
4 tablespoons butter or margarine
3 tablespoons flour
1½ teaspoons salt
⅛ teaspoon pepper
2 cups milk

In a large saucepan, cook chopped carrots until tender. In a skillet, fry onions in butter until a light yellow, add flour, salt, and pepper and blend; add mixture to carrots and mix thoroughly; add milk and cook over medium heat 3 minutes, stirring constantly. Press through a coarse sieve, reheat, and serve hot. Serves 4 to 6.

CARRATO SOUP

4 medium potatoes, pared and sliced
3 large carrots, sliced
1 medium onion, peeled and sliced
2 cups water
1 tablespoon melted butter or margarine
1 tablespoon flour
2 cups milk
salt and pepper to taste

Boil vegetables in water until very tender, rub through a coarse sieve, and return sieved vegetables to water. In a small saucepan, make a thin white sauce with butter, flour, milk, salt, and pepper over low heat, then add to sieved vegetables and water. Blend all thoroughly, bring to a boil, then serve. Serves 6.

CAROLINA CAULIFLOWER SOUP

1 medium cauliflower, cut coarsely
4 cups water
2 cups milk, scalded
4 tablespoons butter or margarine
2 tablespoons onion, chopped
3 tablespoons flour
2 teaspoons salt
dash cayenne pepper

In a large saucepan, cook the cauliflower in 4 cups boiling water until very soft; rub cauliflower through a coarse sieve into the water; reduce heat and add milk. In a large skillet, melt butter, then add onion and fry until tender. Blend in flour, salt, and cayenne; then add cauliflower-milk mixture gradually, raise heat to high, and stir constantly, cooking for 5 minutes. Serves 6.

CREAM OF CELERY SOUP

2 cups celery, minced
1 teaspoon onion, minced
4 cups warm milk
3 tablespoons butter or margarine
3 tablespoons flour
1½ teaspoons salt
½ teaspoon pepper

In a large skillet, cook celery and onion in boiling, salted water until tender; drain off water. Melt butter in skillet, then blend in flour, salt, pepper, and 1 cup milk; cook over low heat for 5 minutes, stirring constantly. Add remainder of milk and bring to a near boil, stirring constantly, then serve immediately. Serves 6.

CELERY CHOWDER

4 cups celery, diced
1 small onion, minced
1 cup carrots, thinly sliced
2 tablespoons butter or margarine
1 tablespoon flour
2 teaspoons salt
¼ teaspoon pepper
3 cups milk, scalded

In a large saucepan, cook celery in salted, boiling water until tender; drain off water and rub celery through a coarse sieve, returning to pan. In a skillet, fry onion and carrots in butter until browned lightly, then combine with sieved celery. Raise to medium heat, blend in flour, salt, and pepper. Gradually add milk, stirring constantly. Raise heat to high and cook 3 minutes, stirring constantly. Serves 6.

CORN SOUP

1 cup corn kernels
2 cups boiling water
2 tablespoons butter or margarine
2 tablespoons flour
½ teaspoon salt
⅛ teaspoon pepper
1 teaspoon minced onion
2 cups milk

In a large skillet, simmer corn and water together for 20 minutes; drain and press through a coarse sieve and set aside. Melt butter, blend in flour, salt, pepper, and onion; add milk gradually. Heat to boiling, stirring constantly, and add sieved corn. Reduce heat to medium and cook, stirring constantly, until thickened, about 5 minutes. Serves 4.

CORN SOUP CANADIENNE

2 cups corn, grated
1 cup boiling water
1 tablespoon onion, grated
2 tablespoons butter or margarine
2 tablespoons flour
3 cups brown stock
1 teaspoon salt
¼ teaspoon pepper

In a large saucepan, cook corn and onion in boiling water 15 minutes; strain and set aside. Melt butter and stir in flour, blending thoroughly. Add stock, salt, and pepper and cook over medium heat for 5 minutes. Stir in corn pulp and cook 10 minutes, stirring occasionally. Serves 4 to 6.

CORN'MATER CHOWDER

2 cups corn kernels, cooked, drained, and still warm
3 large tomatoes, chopped
1 small onion, chopped
2 cups potatoes, pared and diced
2 tablespoons butter or margarine
salt and pepper to taste
1 tablespoon sugar
1 quart boiling water
1 cup evaporated milk

In a large saucepan, melt butter and fry onion slowly until tender. In alternate layers, add corn, tomatoes, and potatoes; sprinkle with sugar, salt, and pepper, then add boiling water and cook, over medium heat, until potatoes are tender. Remove from heat and add milk slowly, stirring until blended thoroughly. Serves 6.

CORN'TATER CHOWDER

2 cups corn kernels, cooked, drained, and still warm
2 cups potatoes, pared and diced
2 tablespoons onion, diced
2 tablespoons celery, diced
½ teaspoon salt
⅛ teaspoon pepper
1½ cups boiling water
2 cups milk, scalded
1 tablespoon flour
1 tablespoon cold water

Combine corn, potatoes, onion, celery, salt, pepper, and boiling water in a large saucepan and cook over medium heat until potatoes are tender. Blend in scalded milk and thicken mixture with flour mixed with water; bring to a boil and serve at once. Serves 6.

CORN CHOWDER

1 cup corn kernels, cooked, drained, and still warm
2 tablespoons butter or margarine
1 large onion, diced
3 cups potatoes, cooked, pared, and diced
2 cups boiling water
4 cups milk, scalded
½ teaspoon salt
dash pepper

In a skillet, fry onion in butter until tender. In a large saucepan, combine onion, corn, potatoes, boiling water and hot milk and cook over medium heat 5 minutes, stirring constantly. Raise heat and bring to near boiling, then serve at once. Serves 6 to 8.

DELAWARE EGGPLANT SOUP

1 large eggplant, diced
2 large tomatoes, quartered
1 teaspoon chopped chives
3 tablespoons butter or margarine
1 cup brown stock
2 cups boiling water
1 teaspoon minced parsley
¼ teaspoon salt
¼ teaspoon sugar
dash cayenne pepper

Melt butter in a large skillet and fry vegetables for 10 minutes. Combine vegetables and remaining ingredients in a large saucepan, heat to boiling, then reduce heat and simmer until eggplant is tender, about 40 minutes. Serves 4.

EASY GARDEN SOUP

1 carrot, diced
½ small turnip, pared and diced
⅓ cup cabbage, chopped
1 tablespoon butter or margarine
3 cups brown stock
½ leek, sliced (2 whole scallions may be substituted)
½ cup peas
½ large potato, pared and diced
salt to taste
1 teaspoon minced paraley

Fry carrot, turnip, and cabbage in butter until tender, then combine with remainder of ingredients in a large saucepan and bring to a boil. Reduce heat and simmer, covered, for 40 minutes. Serves 4 to 6.

JERUSALEM CREAM SOUP

2 cups Jerusalem artichokes, pared and sliced
3 cups water
2 tablespoons butter or margarine
2 tablespoons flour
1 teaspoon salt
⅛ teaspoon pepper
1 cup evaporated milk
1 cup milk

In a large saucepan, cook artichokes in boiling water, covered, for about 10 minutes or until very soft. Rub through a coarse sieve, retaining liquid, and return to saucepan. Add remaining ingredients and blend thoroughly; gradually bring to a boil, stirring constantly, and cook 3 minutes. Serve at once. Serves 6.

CREAM OF CUCUMBER SOUP

4 cucumbers, pared and chopped
1 cup celery, chopped
2 tablespoons onion, chopped
1 tablespoon green pepper, minced
4 tablespoons butter or margarine
2 tablespoons flour
1 teaspoon salt
dash pepper
4 cups milk
1 cup evaporated milk

In a skillet in a small amount of water, cook covered vegetables 20 minutes over low heat or until tender. In a large saucepan, combine cooked vegetables, butter, flour, salt, pepper, and milk. Cook over medium heat for 10 minutes, stirring constantly until thickened. Press mixture through a coarse sieve, add evaporated milk, return to heat, and heat to a boil. Serve at once. Serves 6.

JULIENNE SOUP

2 cups carrots, diced
1 cup turnips, pared and diced
¾ cup celery, thinly sliced
1 teaspoon salt
½ teaspoon pepper
2 quarts brown stock
salt and pepper to taste

In a large saucepan, combine carrots, turnips, celery, salt, and pepper with just enough water to cover; bring water to a boil, cover pan, and cook until very tender; drain. Combine vegetables, stock, salt, and pepper in the saucepan; bring to a boil; reduce heat and simmer 10 minutes. Serves 8 to 10.

LETTUCE SOUP

1½ cups lettuce, chopped fine
2 medium onions, diced
1 large tomato, diced
1 cup celery, chopped
1½ quarts cold water
1 pint brown stock
2 teaspoons salt
¼ teaspoon pepper
1 bay leaf
1 cup beet tops or mustard greens, chopped fine

Combine all ingredients at once in a large saucepan and bring to a boil; boil 5 minutes. Reduce heat and simmer 40 minutes. Serves 8 to 10.

CREAM OF LETTUCE SOUP

1 large head lettuce, chopped coarsely
3 tablespoons water
4 cups white stock
2 tablespoons butter or margarine
2 tablespoons flour
½ teaspoon salt
¼ teaspoon pepper
2 cups hot milk

Cook lettuce in water in a large, covered saucepan until very tender; rub lettuce through a coarse sieve, retaining liquid, and return to sauce pan. Add all ingredients but milk to saucepan and cook over medium heat 10 minutes, blending thoroughly. Gradually stir in milk and bring to a boil. Serve at once. Serves 6.

CREAM OF LIMA BEAN SOUP

2½ cups lima beans
1 quart cold water
2 tablespoons butter or margarine
1 small onion, diced
¼ cup carrot, thinly sliced
2 tablespoons flour
1 teaspoon salt
½ teaspoon pepper
½ teaspoon paprika
dash Tabasco sauce
2 cups milk, scalded

In a large saucepan, cook beans and water together until beans are very tender; then rub through a coarse sieve, retaining liquid, and return to saucepan. In a skillet, melt butter and fry onion and carrot until tender; blend in flour, salt, pepper, paprika, and Tabasco sauce; add to bean mixture. Gradually add milk. Heat to boiling, stirring constantly, and serve at once. Serves 6 to 8.

QUICK MINESTRONE

1 cup tender cabbage, finely chopped
1 cup corn kernels
1 cup green beans, cut into 1-inch pieces
1 cup lima beans
1 cup onion, diced
2 large tomatoes, diced
½ clove garlic, minced
salt and pepper to taste
2½ cups brown stock
2 cups water

In a large saucepan, combine ingredients in the order listed, bring to a boil, and cook, covered, for 10 minutes. Reduce heat and simmer 30 minutes. Serves 6 to 8.

SAVANNAH OKRA SOUP

3 cups okra, sliced
2 large tomatoes, peeled and chopped
4 cups cold water
2 beef bouillon cubes
salt and pepper to taste

Combine all ingredients in a large saucepan, bring to a boil, and cook 10 minutes, stirring frequently. Reduce heat and simmer 45 minutes or until thick. Serves 4 to 6.

FRENCH ONION SOUP

4 medium onions, thinly sliced
2 tablespoons butter or margarine
1 quart brown stock
½ teaspoon Worcestershire sauce
salt and pepper to taste
grated Parmesan cheese

In a large saucepan, brown the onions lightly in butter, then add stock, Worcestershire, salt, and pepper and simmer 30 minutes or until onions are tender. Serve sprinkled with Parmesan cheese. Serves 4.

PURÉE OF ONION SOUP

6 small onions, peeled
2 cups boiling water
2 tablespoons butter or margarine
2 tablespoons flour
1 teaspoon salt
⅛ teaspoon pepper
2 cups white stock
2 cups milk, scalded

In a large skillet, cook the onions, covered, in the water until very tender; drain and force onions through a sieve, putting sieved onions in a large saucepan. Melt the butter in the skillet and blend in flour, salt, and pepper; gradually blend in stock and milk; cook over medium heat 5 minutes, stirring constantly. Pour liquid onto sieved onion, blend thoroughly, and cooknover medium heat another 5 minutes, stirring constantly. Serves 6.

CREAM OF ONION SOUP

6 medium onions, sliced
3 tablespoons butter or margarine
3 tablespoons flour
1 teaspoon salt
¼ teaspoon pepper
4 cups hot milk

In a large saucepan, cover onions with water and boil until tender; drain and rub through a coarse sieve and set aside. Melt butter in saucepan, blend in flour, salt, and pepper, and blend thoroughly. Add milk and sieved onion gradually, stirring frequently. Bring to a boil and cook 3 minutes, stirring constantly. Serves 6.

ONION SOUP GRATINÉE

3 medium onions, thinly sliced
3 tablespoons butter or margarine
3 pints brown stock
1 teaspoon salt
dash pepper
1 small clove garlic, minced
2 tablespoons chopped parsley
⅓ loaf French bread
4 tablespoons grated Romano cheese

In a large saucepan, simmer onions in butter until soft and lightly browned; add stock and boil 10 minutes; then add salt, pepper, garlic, and parsley and cook over medium heat another 10 minutes, stirring frequently. Cut bread into thin slices and dry them in a warm oven a few minutes. Pour the soup into a deep casserole, float bread slices on top, and sprinkle with grated cheese. Set casserole in a hot (500°F) oven long enough to brown cheese. Serves 6 to 8.

PEAPICKERS' ONION AND PEA SOUP

2 medium onions, thinly sliced
2 tablespoons butter or margarine
2½ cups brown stock
1 cup peas, finely chopped
1 cup evaporated milk
¼ teaspoon salt
dash pepper

Fry onions in butter in a large saucepan until light brown. Combine remaining ingredients and bring to a boil. Reduce heat and simmer, covered, 10 minutes, stirring occasionally. Serves 6.

GREEN PEA SOUP

4 cups peas
¼ cup celery, diced
1 medium onion, thinly sliced
1 small turnip, pared and diced
2 cups brown stock
1 quart water
1 tablespoon water
1 tablespoon butter or margarine
1 teaspoon salt
¼ teaspoon pepper
½ teaspoon sugar

Combine all vegetables, stock, and water in a large saucepan and cook, covered, over medium heat until turnips are tender; rub through a coarse sieve, retaining liquid, and return to saucepan. Thoroughly blend in remaining ingredients and bring to a boil; reduce heat and simmer for 15 minutes. Serves 6.

CREAM OF PEA SOUP

2 cups peas, cooked, drained, and still warm
¼ cup water
½ teaspoon onion juice
3 tablespoons butter or margarine
¼ cup flour
2 teaspoons salt
¼ teaspoon pepper
4 cups milk, scalded

Cook peas, water, and onion juice in a large saucepan, covered, over medium heat for 15 minutes; rub all through a coarse sieve and set aside. Melt the butter in a saucepan over low heat and blend in flour, salt, and pepper; add the milk gradually, stirring constantly. Add sieved peas and heat until boiling, stirring constantly. Serves 6.

PARSNIP CHOWDER

1½ cups parsnips, pared and diced
1 medium onion, diced
2 cups potatoes, pared and diced
2 tablespoons butter or margarine
3 cups boiling water
1 teaspoon salt
¼ teaspoon pepper
4 cups milk, scalded
1 tablespoon vegetable oil

In a large saucepan, fry onion in butter until browned lightly. Add parsnips, potatoes, boiling water, salt, and pepper and simmer, covered, until vegetables are tender. Raise heat to high and blend in milk and oil thoroughly, stirring constantly. Serves 6 to 8.

GREAT GRATED POTATO SOUP

6 medium potatoes, pared and grated
1 leek, thinly sliced
1 small onion, minced
½ clove garlic, thinly sliced
1 tablespoon butter or margarine
6 cups brown stock
salt and pepper to taste

Melt butter in a large saucepan and cook garlic slowly for 5 minutes; remove garlic. Add remainder of ingredients and boil, covered, for 5 minutes. Reduce heat, remove cover, and simmer 20 minutes. Serves 6 to 8.

PENNSYLVANIA POTATO SOUP

8 medium potatoes, pared, cooked, drained, and finely chopped
1 quart milk
salt and pepper to taste
2 tablespoons butter or margarine
½ cup flour
¼ cup milk
1 egg, beaten well

Combine milk and potatoes in a large saucepan and cook over medium heat 5 minutes, stirring constantly; add salt and pepper, stir, and remove from heat. In a small saucepan, melt butter and blend in flour, milk, and egg, mixing all thoroughly. Drop mixture by teaspoonfuls into potato-milk mixture, cover, and cook over low heat for 10 minutes. Serve at once. Serves 4.

CREAMY POTATO SOUP

2 large potatoes, pared and diced
1⅓ cups boiling water
1 teaspoon salt
1 small onion, sliced
½ teaspoon pepper
2 cups sour cream

Combine first 5 ingredients and boil, covered, for 12 minutes. Reduce heat to medium, blend in sour cream, and cook 10 minutes, stirring constantly. Serve at once. Serves 6.

CABBAGE POTAGE

3 large potatoes, pared and diced
2 cups tender cabbage, chopped fine
1 small onion, chopped
2 tablespoons butter or margarine
3 cups water
1 teaspoon salt
1½ cups evaporated milk
paprika

In a large saucepan, melt butter and fry onion until just tender. Add potatoes, cabbage, water, and salt and cook covered, over low heat, until potatoes are tender. Stir in milk and heat to near boiling. Sprinkle with paprika and serve at once. Serves 6.

LEEKY POTATO SOUP

2 medium potatoes, pared and diced
1 cup leeks, sliced
3 tablespoons butter or margarine
4 cups cold water
1 bay leaf
2 tablespoons tomato catsup
½ small onion, grated
¼ cup celery, chopped
2 tablespoons parsley, minced
1 teaspoon salt
⅛ teaspoon pepper
1 cup milk

Melt butter in a large saucepan and cook sliced leeks over low heat 5 minutes but do not brown. Add water, bay leaf, and catsup; cover and simmer for 15 minutes. Add potatoes, onion, celery, parsley, salt, and pepper and cook covered, over low heat, until potatoes are soft. Add milk and heat to near boiling, stirring constantly, then serve at once. Serves 4.

SOUTHERN POTATO SOUP

6 medium potatoes, pared and diced
1 medium onion, sliced
6 medium tomatoes, diced
1 turnip, pared and diced
2 cups peas
1 carrot, grated
¼ cup uncooked rice
1 tablespoon salt
1 tablespoon sugar
½ teaspoon pepper
dash allspice
2 quarts brown stock

Arrange vegetables, rice, and seasonings in alternate layers in a shallow baking dish, then pour stock over vegetables. Cover and set dish in a pan of hot water and bake in a 300°F oven for at least 5 hours. Serves 8.

SARGASSO SOUP

3 large potatoes, pared and diced
2 cups spinach, finely chopped
1 small onion, chopped
2 tablespoons butter or margarine

3 cups water
1 teaspoon salt
⅛ teaspoon pepper
1½ cups evaporated milk

In a large saucepan, melt butter and fry onion until just tender. Add potatoes, spinach, water, salt, and pepper and cook, covered, over low heat until potatoes are soft. Stir in milk and bring to a near boil. Serve at once. Serves 6.

SIOUX CITY SQUASH SOUP

2 cups summer squash, sliced, cooked, and drained
1 small onion, thinly sliced
4 cups milk
1 small bay leaf, crumbled
3 tablespoons butter or margarine
3 tablespoons flour
1 teaspoon salt
¼ teaspoon celery salt
dash cayenne pepper

Scald milk with onion and bay leaf in a large saucepan; strain, returning milk to pan, and discard onion and bay leaf. Add remainder of ingredients, including squash, and cook over medium heat 5 minutes, stirring constantly. Serve at once. Serves 6.

TAMPA TOMATO SOUP

3 large tomatoes, chopped
¼ cup onion, diced
¼ cup carrot, diced
¼ cup celery, diced
4 tablespoons butter or margarine
1 teaspoon salt
¼ teaspoon pepper
1 small bay leaf
⅛ teaspoon ground cloves
1 quart brown stock

In a large saucepan, fry onion, carrot, and celery in butter for 5 minutes. Add all ingredients and cook over low heat, covered, for 35 minutes. Rub mixture through a coarse sieve, return to saucepan, and add stock. Bring to a boil, stirring frequently, and serve at once. Serves 6 to 8.

CREAM OF SPINACH SOUP

1 pound spinach, chopped coarsely
2 tablespoons water
4 cups white stock
2 tablespoons butter or margarine
2 tablespoons flour
½ teaspoon salt
¼ teaspoon pepper
2 cups hot milk

Put spinach and water in a large, covered saucepan and cook over medium heat until soft; press spinach through a sieve and return to saucepan. Add stock, butter, flour, salt, and pepper and blend thoroughly; cook over medium heat 5 minutes. Add milk gradually, bring to a near boil, stirring constantly, and serve at once. Serves 6 to 8.

CREAM OF TOMATO SOUP

3 large tomatoes, chopped
3 tablespoons water
1 tablespoon onion, minced
1 teaspoon salt
¼ teaspoon pepper
dash cayenne pepper
2 teaspoons sugar
2 tablespoons butter or margarine
2 tablespoons flour
1 quart milk, scalded

Cook tomatoes, water, onion, salt, pepper, cayenne, and sugar in a large saucepan over low heat, covered, for 15 minutes; rub through a coarse sieve and set aside. Melt butter in saucepan over medium heat and blend in flour; add milk gradually, stirring constantly. Add sieved tomato mixture and bring to a boil, stirring constantly. Serves 6.

TURNIP TUREEN

2 cups cooked, drained, mashed turnips
1 cup cooked, drained, mashed potatoes
2 tablespoons butter or margarine
3 cups water
1 teaspoon salt
1½ cups evaporated milk
paprika

Combine first 5 ingredients in a large saucepan and cook over medium heat 10 minutes, blending thoroughly. Cover and simmer for 10 minutes. Raise heat to high, stir in milk, and bring to a near boil, stirring constantly. Serve at once. Serves 6.

VEGETABLE SOUP

1 cup lima beans
1 large potato, pared and diced
2 large tomatoes, diced
1 cup corn, grated
1 cup tender cabbage, chopped very fine
1 large turnip, pared and diced
1 large carrot, diced
1 small onion, chopped
1 cup peas
salt and pepper to taste
2 quarts brown stock

Combine all ingredients at once in a large saucepan and bring to a boil. Reduce heat and simmer until vegetables are tender, stirring occasionally. Serves 8 to 10.

WEST VIRGINIA VEGETABLE CHOWDER

2 cups potatoes, pared and diced
1 cup carrots, diced
1 medium onion, diced
1 medium green pepper, diced
3 tablespoons butter or margarine
2 tablespoons flour
2 cups milk
2 large tomatoes, chopped
1 teaspoon salt
¼ teaspoon pepper
1 quart plus 1 cup brown stock

Place potatoes and carrots with stock in a large saucepan and cook over medium heat, covered, until tender. In a skillet, fry onion and green pepper in butter for 5 minutes, but do not brown; add flour and blend; add milk and cook over medium heat 5 minutes, stirring constantly until smooth. Pour milk mixture over vegetables and stock and mix thoroughly. Cook over medium heat 5 minutes, stirring constantly, and serve at once. Serves 6 to 8.

STEWS, CASSEROLES
AND
COMBINATION DISHES

BEAN AND BROCCOLI CUSTARD CASSEROLE
½ pound green beans, cut into 1-inch pieces, cooked, and drained
½ pound yellow (wax) beans, cut into 1-inch pieces, cooked, and
　　drained
½ large head broccoli, chopped coarsely, cooked, and drained
1 scallion, minced
2 tablespoons butter or margarine
2 tablespoons flour
1 cup milk
½ cup mayonnaise
2 eggs, beaten well
salt and pepper to taste

Melt butter in a large saucepan, then blend in flour and milk and stir until smooth. Over low heat, add scallion, salt, pepper, eggs, and mayonnaise, blending all until smooth. Add beans and broccoli, mix well, then turn all into a buttered, deep baking dish. Place in a pan of hot water and bake at 375°F for 25 minutes or until custard is set. Serves 6.

CABBAGE-PEA COMBO
3 cups cabbage, shredded, cooked, and drained
1 cup peas, cooked and drained
2 tablespoons butter or margarine
salt and pepper to taste
¼ cup whipping cream

Melt butter in a large saucepan, then add salt, pepper, and whipping cream, cooking over low heat and stirring until blended. Add cabbage, mix well, raise heat to medium, and cook for 3 minutes, stirring frequently. Top with peas and serve at once. Serves 4.

CABBAGE STROGANOFF
½ large head cabbage, chopped
1 small onion, chopped
¾ cup butter or margarine
8 ounces egg noodles, cooked and drained
2 tablespoons poppy seeds
1 teaspoon salt
pepper to taste

In a large skillet, melt half the butter and cook the cabbage and onion over medium-high heat until tender and lightly browned. Add hot noodles, poppy seeds, salt, pepper, and remainder of butter and mix all thoroughly. Cook, stirring, over medium heat for 3 minutes. Serve at once. Serves 4.

THREE Cs CASSEROLE

3 cups cauliflower flowers, sliced, cooked, and drained
3 cups carrots, sliced, cooked, and drained
2 tablespoons butter or margarine
2 tablespoons flour
⅛ teaspoon mild prepared mustard
½ cup warm water
½ cup whipping cream
salt and pepper to taste
⅔ cup grated mild Cheddar cheese

Melt butter in a large saucepan, then blend in flour until smooth. Over low heat, add mustard, water, whipping cream, salt, and pepper, blending all until smooth; add cheese last, stirring until smooth. Stir in vegetables, then turn mixture into a buttered, deep baking dish and bake at 300°F for 20 minutes. Serves 6 to 8.

CARROTS AND PEAS

2 large carrots, cut into 1-inch pieces
1 cup peas
2 cups boiling water
3 tablespoons butter or margarine
2 tablespoons flour

In a large saucepan, cook carrots, covered, in boiling water 5 minutes; add peas and cook, covered, until peas and carrots are tender. Drain, reserving ½ cup liquid, and set vegetables aside. Melt the butter in the saucepan and blend in flour until smooth; add ½ cup liquid and cook over medium heat, stirring constantly until smooth. Add carrots and peas, mix well, reduce heat, and simmer for 5 minutes. Serve at once. Serves 3 to 4.

KENTUCKY CARROT STEW

2 cups carrots, cut into ½-inch pieces
1 large potato, pared and diced
1 large turnip, pared and diced
4 scallions, thinly sliced
2 tablespoons butter or margarine
2 tablespoons flour
2 cups water reserved from vegetables
1 tablespoon sugar
1 teaspoon salt
¼ teaspoon white pepper

Boil vegetables in a large saucepan in 3 cups of water until tender; drain and set aside. In a large skillet, melt butter and blend in flour, then stir in water, sugar, salt, and pepper, blending thoroughly. Add vegetables and simmer, covered, for 20 minutes. Serves 4.

COLCAMON

2 cups kale, chopped (cabbage may be substituted)
2 cups hot mashed potatoes
2 scallions, thinly sliced
1 cup milk
salt and pepper to taste
dash mace
about ⅓ cup melted butter or margarine

Cook the kale in boiling water in a large saucepan until tender; drain. In a skillet, simmer scallions in milk until tender. Add milk, scallions, potatoes, salt, pepper, and mace to kale and mix thoroughly. Cook covered, over low heat, for 3 minutes. Make a well in the middle of the mixture and pour in melted butter. Serve at once. Serves 4 to 6.

(*Note:* any leftover mixture can be fried as patties in butter or bacon fat until browned on both sides.)

CUCUMBER AND TOMATO CASSEROLE

2 medium cucumbers, pared, thinly sliced, cooked, and drained
2 medium tomatoes, thinly sliced
salt and pepper to taste
3 tablespoons butter or margarine
2 tablespoons flour
¾ cup milk
⅓ cup plus 3 tablespoons grated Parmesan cheese

Place cucumbers in the bottom of a buttered shallow baking dish and sprinkle with salt and pepper. Melt butter in a small saucepan over low heat, then blend in flour, stirring until thickened. Add milk and cook until thickened, stirring frequently. Add ⅓ cup cheese and stir until cheese melts and mixture is smooth. Pour mixture over cucumbers, place tomatoes on top, and sprinkle with 3 tablespoons cheese. Bake at 350°F for 20 minutes or until top is browned. Serves 4.

CORN AND TOMATO BAKE

3 cups corn kernels
5 large tomatoes, sliced
¼ pound butter or margarine
½ cup unseasoned bread crumbs
salt and pepper to taste

Butter a deep casserole and place in layers, beginning with corn, corn and tomatoes until vegetables are used. Sprinkle bread crumbs, pieces of butter, salt, and pepper on top. Bake, covered, 20 minutes at 375°F; remove cover and bake 15 more minutes. Serves 4 to 6.

SATURDAY-NIGHT SPECIAL

1 medium eggplant, diced
1½ cups okra, sliced
1 small onion, chopped
2 large, ripe tomatoes, diced
5 tablespoons vegetable oil
1 tablespoon butter or margarine
1 teaspoon salt
¼ teaspoon pepper

Combine all ingredients at once in a large saucepan and mix well. Simmer, covered, until eggplant is tender. Serves 6.

FENNEL AND TOMATOES

2 large fennel bulbs, cooked, drained, and diced
2 large tomatoes, diced
1 tablespoon onion, grated
1 tablespoon fennel leaves, chopped
1 teaspoon salt
1 teaspoon sugar
½ teaspoon paprika
½ teaspoon pepper

Arrange fennel and tomatoes on the bottom of a buttered shallow baking dish. Sprinkle with onion, leaves, salt, sugar, paprika, and pepper and bake at 325°F for 20 minutes. Serves 4.

GREEN AND WHITE TOSS

4 medium peppers, diced, cooked, and drained
3 medium potatoes, pared, cooked, drained, and diced
1 small onion, chopped
¼ pound butter or margarine
1 teaspoon lemon juice
1 teaspoon salt
¼ teaspoon pepper
¼ teaspoon curry powder
⅓ cup grated mild Cheddar cheese

Melt butter in a small saucepan, then blend in lemon juice, salt, pepper, and curry powder; add onion, cover, and simmer until onion is tender. Mix pepper and potato pieces together, then turn into a buttered deep baking dish. Pour butter-onion sauce over all, then sprinkle top with grated cheese. Bake at 300°F for 30 minutes. Serves 6.

ITALIAN CASSEROLE

1 medium eggplant, pared and sliced
2 medium zucchinis, sliced
1 large green pepper, sliced
1 large onion, sliced
3 large tomatoes, diced
1 small clove garlic, minced
½ cup olive or vegetable oil
1½ teaspoons oregano
1 teaspoon sugar
½ teaspoon salt
pepper to taste

Cook eggplant, zucchinis, pepper, onion, and garlic in hot oil in a large ovenproof skillet until just tender. Sprinkle with oregano, sugar, salt, and pepper; add tomatoes and stir a few times. Bake at 350°F for 25 minutes. Serves 6.

CARROT AND PARSNIP BAKE

1½ cups parsnips, diced
1½ cups carrots, thinly sliced
1 tablespoon onion, minced
⅔ cup water
3 tablespoons butter or margarine
salt and pepper to taste

Combine all ingredients at once in a large skillet and simmer, covered, until parsnips are tender. Serves 6.

MEXICALI SURPRISE

1 large green pepper, sliced
2½ cups corn kernels, cooked and drained
2 large tomatoes, chopped
1 tablespoon onion, minced
3 tablespoons butter or margarine
1 tablespoon milk
salt and pepper to taste

Melt butter in a large skillet, add pepper and onion, and simmer until tender. Add corn, tomatoes, milk, salt, and pepper; raise heat to medium and cook, stirring frequently, until thoroughly warmed. Serves 4.

JENNY'S LIMA AND TOMATO CASSEROLE

1½ cups limas, cooked and drained
2 large tomatoes, chopped
1 teaspoon chopped chives
⅛ teaspoon garlic salt
3 tablespoons olive or vegetable oil
1 teaspoon oregano

Toss first five ingredients together thoroughly, place in a shallow baking dish, and sprinkle with oregano. Bake, covered, at 350°F for 20 minutes. Remove cover and bake until top is slightly browned, about 10 minutes. Serves 4 to 6.

MINNESOTA POTPOURRI

3 cups peas, cooked and drained
1 cuz pea liquid
1 dozen scallions, sliced
3 tablespoons butter or margarine
1 tablespoon flour
1 tablespoon sugar
1 teaspoon salt
pepper to taste

Simmer scallions in butter in a large skillet until just tender. Blend in flour, sugar, salt, and pepper, mixing all well. Raise heat to medium, add peas and liquid, and cook, stirring frequently, until thickened. Serve at once. Serves 4 to 6.

POTATO MASHEROLE

2 cups mashed potatoes at room temperature
1 tablespoon chopped chives
4 scallion bulbs, thinly sliced
2 eggs, beaten
1 4-ounce package cream cheese, softened
1 tablespoon flour
½ teaspoon salt
¼ teaspoon pepper

Combine all ingredients at once except chives and blend thoroughly. Turn mixture into a buttered, shallow baking dish, then sprinkle with chives. Bake at 300°F for 40 minutes. Serves 4 to 6.

POTATO-TOMATO BAKE

3 large tomatoes, sliced
2 medium potatoes, pared and chopped
2 scallions, sliced thinly
1 tablespoon butter or margarine
¼ cup unseasoned bread crumbs
¼ cup grated American cheese
salt and pepper to taste

Mix vegetables with salt and pepper and place half the mixture in a buttered deep baking dish. Sprinkle bread crumbs, then cheese, onto mixture; add remainder of vegetables. Bake, covered, at 375°F for 20 minutes. Remove cover and bake at 325°F for 10 minutes. Serve at once. Serves 4.

SEMINOLE SUCCOTASH

1½ cups corn kernels, cooked and drained
1½ cups lima beans, cooked and drained
2 scallion tops, chopped
5 tablespoons butter or margarine
⅔ cup whipping cream
salt and pepper to taste

Melt butter in a large skillet and add corn, limas, scallions, salt, and pepper; cook over medium heat for 3 minutes, stirring frequently. Stir in cream and cook another 3 minutes, stirring constantly. Serves 4 to 6.

SPINACH CASSEROLE

2 pounds spinach, chopped
2 tablespoons melted butter or margarine
¾ cup milk
salt and pepper to taste
1 teaspoon chopped chives or minced onion
¼ cup grated Parmesan cheese
2 eggs, beaten

Drop spinach into a few tablespoonsful of salted, boiling water in a large saucepan and cook for 1 minute only; drain well. Add remaining ingredients in order listed, blend thoroughly, and cook for 1 minute over medium heat, stirring constantly. Pour mixture into a shallow baking dish and bake at 350°F for 25 minutes. Serves 4.

SOUTHERN-STYLE TOMATOES

1½ pounds okra, sliced
3 large tomatoes, diced
1 small onion, chopped
3 tablespoons butter or margarine
1 tablespoon water
1 teaspoon salt
½ teaspoon pepper
dash cayenne pepper

Combine all ingredients except butter in a large skillet and cook, covered, over medium heat for 5 minutes. Remove cover, add butter, raise heat to high, and cook another 3 minutes, turning and stirring frequently. Serves 6.

TOMATOES TOLEDO

1 medium eggplant, sliced
3 large tomatoes, sliced
1 teaspoon onion, minced
1 tablespoon water
1 tablespoon olive or vegetable oil
1 teaspoon sugar
½ teaspoon salt
¼ teaspoon pepper

Combine water and oil in a large skillet and cook eggplant slices, covered, over medium heat until just tender. Remove cover, add sugar, salt, pepper, and tomatoes, raise heat to high, and cook, turning frequently, until vegetables begin to brown. Serves 6.

EASY SICILIAN CASSEROLE

6 large tomatoes, quartered
3 tablespoons olive or vegetable oil
⅔ cup seasoned bread crumbs
salt and pepper to taste
2 tablespoons grated Parmesan cheese

Spread half the oil on the bottom of a deep baking dish. Sprinkle half of the bread crumbs onto oil. Arrange tomatoes on bread crumbs. Cover tomatoes with remainder of bread crumbs, then sprinkle with oil, salt and pepper, and cheese. Bake, covered, at 350°F for 30 minutes. Remove cover and bake another 20 minutes until top is well browned. Serves 4 to 6.

CELERY-TOMATO SIMMER

2 cups celery, cut into ½-inch pieces
2 large tomatoes, diced
1 teaspoon onion, minced
3 tablespoons butter or margarine
½ teaspoon salt
pepper to taste
1 tablespoon water

Melt butter in a large saucepan and add celery, onion, salt, pepper, and water; simmer, covered, for 5 minutes. Add tomatoes, stir a few times, and simmer, covered, until celery is tender. Serves 4.

TOMATOES AND CUKES

3 large tomatoes, sliced
2 medium cucumbers, peeled and sliced thinly
2 scallions, sliced
3 tablespoons butter or margarine
½ teaspoon salt
½ teaspoon sugar
pepper to taste

Melt butter in a large skillet, add scallions and cook over low heat for 3 minutes. Add cucumber slices, salt, sugar, and pepper, raise heat to medium, and cook, turning frequently, another 3 minutes. Place tomato slices on top, reduce heat, and simmer until tomatoes are warmed through. Serves 4 to 6.

LAYERED TOMATO-EGGPLANT CASSEROLE

1 large eggplant, pared and sliced into ¼-inch slices
3 large tomatoes, peeled and chopped
1 tablespoon chopped chives
1 teaspoon salt
1 tablespoon flour
1 tablespoon water
1 tablespoon sugar
¼ teaspoon paprika
½ teaspoon oregano
⅛ teaspoon pepper
⅓ cup grated Parmesan cheese
olive or vegetable oil

In a large saucepan, blend flour and water over low heat. Add tomatoes, chives, salt, sugar, paprika, oregano, and pepper and bring to a boil, stirring frequently; reduce heat and simmer, covered, for 10 minutes. In a large skillet, cook eggplant slices in hot oil until tender and lightly browned. Layer the bottom of a deep casserole with half the eggplant slices, then cover with half the tomato mixture; repeat; sprinkle top with cheese. Bake at 375°F for 25 minutes. Serves 4 to 6.

HOLIDAY HASH

3 large beets, cooked, drained, pared, and chopped
2 large potatoes, cooked, drained, pared and chopped
½ teaspoon vegetable oil
1 tablespoon sweet cream
salt and pepper to taste
3 tablespoons butter or margarine

Combine beets, potatoes, oil, cream, salt, and pepper in a large bowl; mix thoroughly. In a large skillet, melt butter and cook mixture over medium-high heat, turning frequently, until browned. Serve at once. Serves 4.

VEGETABLE QUINTET

2 large potatoes, cooked, drained, pared, and chopped
1 large beet, cooked, drained, pared, and chopped
1 large carrot, cooked, drained, and chopped
1 small onion, grated
1 small green pepper, minced
salt and pepper to taste
⅔ cup sweet cream
¼ pound butter or margarine

Combine all ingredients except butter in a large bowl and mix thoroughly. Melt butter in a large skillet and add mixture; simmer, covered, for 5 minutes. Remove cover, raise heat to medium-high, and cook until browned, turning frequently. Serve at once. Serves 4 to 6.

QUICK, THICK STEW

½ medium head cauliflower, broken into small pieces
1 cup peas
½ pound asparagus, cut into 2-inch pieces
3 large carrots, cut into 1-inch pieces
2 beef bouillon cubes
2¾ cups water
5 tablespoons flour
5 tablespoons cold water
2 teaspoons salt
pepper to taste

In a large saucepan, boil 2¾ cups water and bouillon cubes until dissolved. Add vegetables, reduce heat, and simmer, covered, until vegetables are tender. Blend water, salt, and flour until smooth, then stir into vegetables. Stir constantly over low heat until thickened. Serves 6 to 8.

STEWEDEBAKER

3 large carrots, sliced thinly
2 large potatoes, pared and diced
1 large onion, sliced
1 large green pepper, diced
1 small eggplant, pared and diced
1 small zucchini, sliced thinly
1 small crooked-neck squash, sliced thinly
1 garlic clove, minced
1 large tomato, chopped
¼ cup butter or margarine
3½ cups water
salt and pepper to taste

Cook garlic in hot butter in a large skillet for 3 minutes. Add all other ingredients, stir a few times, reduce heat, and simmer, covered, 30 to 35 minutes, or until vegetables are tender. Serves 4 to 6.

ZUCCHINI STEW

3 medium zucchinis, pared and diced
1 large green pepper, diced
1 small clove garlic, minced
2 medium onions, sliced
5 large tomatoes, diced
3 tablespoons olive or vegetable oil
½ cup water
salt and pepper to taste
dash cayenne pepper

In one tablespoon oil, cook tomatoes over medium heat in a large skillet until very soft. Combine tomatoes and remainder of ingredients in a large saucepan, stir a few times, and bring to a boil. Reduce heat and simmer, covered, for 1 hour. Serves 4.

SAUCES, RELISHES
AND
DESSERTS

EASY CUCUMBER DRESSING

1 cup sour cream
salt and pepper to taste
1 teaspoon water
1 cucumber, peeled and finely chopped

Mix sour cream, salt, pepper, and water, then mix in chopped cucumber. Excellent on molded salads. Makes 1½ cups.

CUCUMBER CATSUP

2 large cucumbers
1 small onion
salt and pepper to taste
1 tablespoon sugar
3 tablespoons vinegar

In cold water, thoroughly chill the cucumbers and onion, then pare the cucumbers and grate them into a large bowl; peel the onion and grate it into the cucumbers, then mix. Add salt, pepper, and sugar, then mix in vinegar (more than 3 tablespoons of vinegar may be needed; the consistency should be like jam). Chill before using. Excellent with beef. Makes approximately 2 cups.

RUBY'S RIPE CUCUMBER CATSUP

2 large, very ripe cucumbers, pared, with seed and pulp removed
   and discarded and with meat chopped
1 large onion, peeled and chopped
1 large green pepper, chopped
1 tablespoon mustard seed
2 tablespoons sugar
⅔ cup vinegar

Mix all ingredients thoroughly. Chill before using. Makes approximately 2 cups.

DILL MAYONNAISE

1 cup mayonnaise
1 teaspoon dried dill
1 teaspoon mild prepared mustard
1 tablespoon minced scallion tops
⅛ teaspoon lemon juice
¼ cup heavy whipping cream

Blend first five ingredients, then combine with cream. Makes 1½ cups.

ST. PATRICK'S DAY MAYONNAISE

2 scallions, thinly sliced
10 small spinach leaves
3 tablespoons chopped parsley
1 teaspoon dried tarragon
1 cup mayonnaise
1 cup dairy sour cream
¼ teaspoon Tabasco sauce
⅛ teaspoon lemon juice
salt and pepper to taste

Cook spinach and scallions in boiling, salted water only a few seconds, then drain. In a blender, purée spinach, scallions, tarragon and sour cream. Blend mayonnaise with salt, pepper, Tabasco sauce, and lemon juice, then blend mayonnaise mixture with purée. Makes about 2 cups.

MUSTARD MAYONNAISE

½ cup mayonnaise
1 teaspoon lemon juice
1 teaspoon chopped chives
2 teaspoons mild prepared mustard
2 tablespoons cream

Thoroughly blend all ingredients. Makes ¾ cup.

PEPPER SAUCE

6 large green peppers, sliced
1 medium onion, peeled and sliced
1 clove garlic
½ teaspoon salt
⅔ cup vinegar
½ teaspoon horseradish
½ cup vinegar
1 teaspoon brown sugar
¼ teaspoon ground cloves
¼ teaspoon allspice
¼ teaspoon pepper

Combine first 6 ingredients and boil, uncovered, until onions are very soft, then rub all through a coarse sieve. Mix sieved mixture with remainder of ingredients and return to high heat, boiling and stirring for 5 minutes. Let cool to room temperature then chill. May be used cold or reheated. Makes about ⅔ cup.

TOMATO CATSUP

8 large tomatoes, peeled
½ cup vinegar
2 tablespoons salt
1 teaspoon sugar
½ teaspoon ground cloves
½ teaspoon ginger
½ teaspoon cinnamon
1 teaspoon mustard
1 teaspoon pepper
1 teaspoon allspice
⅛ teaspoon cayenne pepper

In a large skillet, cook the peeled tomatoes in a small amount of unsalted water, covered, until soft; press tomatoes through a sieve. Return sieved tomato mixture to medium heat and add vinegar and salt, stirring constantly; cook for 5 minutes. Add remainder of ingredients and cook, stirring occasionally, until desired thickness is reached. (**Note:** if mixture becomes too thick, a small amount of warm water may be used to thin it). Cool to room temperature, then chill before using. Makes about 1½ cups.

GREEN TOMATO CATSUP

8 large green tomatoes, quartered
1 small onion, peeled and sliced
salt
1 tablespoon mustard seed
1 teaspoon allspice
½ teaspoon ground cloves
1 teaspoon mustard
1 teaspoon pepper
¼ teaspoon ginger
½ teaspoon celery seed
1 tablespoon brown sugar
vinegar to cover

Sprinkle tomatoes and onion with salt; cover and chill in refrigerator overnight. In a large saucepan, combine tomatoes and onions with all ingredients, mixing lightly, then pour in enough vinegar to cover mixture. Boil, uncovered, for at least 45 minutes, stirring occasionally, then press mixture through a coarse sieve. Chill before using. Makes about 1½ cups.

UNCOOKED TOMATO CATSUP

6 large tomatoes, peeled, chopped, and drained
½ cup onion, chopped
½ cup celery, minced
1 tablespoon salt
1 tablespoon sugar
1 teaspoon mustard seed
1 teaspoon cinnamon
1 teaspoon allspice
⅛ teaspoon cayenne pepper
⅓ to ½ cup vinegar

Mix the onion and celery with the drained tomato, then add remainder of ingredients and the amount of vinegar determining the desired consistency. Mix thoroughly. Chill before use. Makes about 1¾ cups.

TOMATO RELISH

2 cups ripe tomatoes, peeled and finely chopped
1 large onion, finely chopped
1 large green pepper, finely chopped
⅓ cup celery, finely chopped
½ cup white vinegar
1 teaspoon mustard seed
¼ cup sugar
1 tablespoon salt

Drain the liquid off the chopped tomatoes, then add remainder of ingredients and mix thoroughly. Refrigerate before use. (**Note:** best if refrigerated for several days). Makes about 1½ pints.

GREEN TOMATO RELISH

2 cups green tomatoes, chopped
1 medium onion, finely chopped
1 medium green pepper, chopped
½ cup white vinegar
1 teaspoon mustard seed
¼ cup sugar
1 tablespoon salt
¼ teaspoon mild prepared mustard

Combine all ingredients and cook, covered, over medium heat for 5 minutes. Let cool, then chill several days before using. Makes about 1½ pints.

CROWN CARROT PIE

1½ cups carrots, pared, cooked, strained, and cooled
1 cup milk
1 cup evaporated milk
2 eggs beaten
1 tablespoon melted butter or margarine
1 teaspoon lemon juice
¾ cup sugar
pastry for bottom of 9-inch pie pan

Add all ingredients to the strained carrots and mix thoroughly, then pour mixture into pastry-lined piepan and bake at 350°F for 40 minutes or until lightly browned.

CARROT PUDDING

1 cup carrots, grated
½ cup potatoes, grated
3 tablespoons melted butter or margarine
1 tablespoon warm water
¾ cup sugar
⅔ cup flour
½ teaspoon baking soda
1 teaspoon nutmeg
1 teaspoon cinnamon
¼ teaspoon ground cloves
¼ teaspoon salt

In a bowl, mix carrots and potatoes. In a saucepan over low heat, melt butter, then add water and remainder of ingredients and cook, stirring, until smooth. Mix butter mixture with carrots and potatoes thoroughly, then turn into a shallow, buttered baking dish and bake, uncovered, for 40 minutes at 350°F or until pudding is set and lightly browned. Serves 4 to 6.

COUNTRY CORN PUDDING

2 cups corn kernels, cooked, drained, and still warm
2 eggs beaten lightly
1 tablespoon sugar
1 teaspoon salt
1½ tablespoons melted butter or margarine
½ teaspoon flour
2 cups scalded milk

Mix all ingredients thoroughly and pour into a shallow, greased 1½-quart baking dish. Set dish in a pan of hot water and bake, uncovered, for about 50 minutes at 350°F or until nicely browned. Serves 4 to 6.

NEW CORN PUDDING

2 cups green corn pulp, uncooked
1⅓ cups milk
1 tablespoon sugar
2 tablespoons butter or margarine
⅛ teaspoon salt
3 eggs, beaten well
1 tablespoon flour

In a saucepan, cook corn pulp, milk, sugar, butter, and salt for 10 minutes over low heat, stirring occasionally. Add eggs and flour last, stirring until blended smoothly. Pour mixture into a buttered, shallow baking dish; set dish in a pan of hot water and bake, uncovered, for 40 minutes at 325°F or until lightly browned. Serves 4 to 6.

EASY EGGPLANT PUDDING

1 medium eggplant, pared and cubed
¾ cup white bread, broken and soaked in 4 tablespoons milk
⅛ teaspoon salt
3 tablespoons sugar
3 eggs, separated

Cook eggplant cubes in salted, boiling water until soft; drain well and mash. Add soaked bread, egg yolks, salt, and sugar; mix thoroughly. Beat egg whites a few times, then mix with eggplant mixture. Bake in a buttered casserole dish, uncovered, for approximately 25 minutes at 350°F or until light crust forms. Serves 4 to 6.

PORTLAND POTATO CAKE

1 cup hot mashed potatoes
2 cups sugar
¼ teaspoon nutmeg
⅛ teaspoon ground cloves
½ teaspoon cinnamon
2¼ cups flour
2 teaspoons baking powder
½ cup melted butter or margarine
4 eggs, lightly beaten
½ cup milk

Mix all ingredients that are dry together first, then add butter, eggs, and milk; last, add the potatoes, blending until smooth. Pour mixture into a greased 10-inch cake pan and bake at 375°F for 25 minutes or until knife blade comes out clean.

FAVORITE JAM PUDDING

2 cups mashed white potatoes, cooled
½ cup melted butter or margarine
3 eggs, slightly beaten
¾ cup sugar
1 cup your favorite jam
¼ teaspoon cinnamon

Combine all ingredients at once and blend thoroughly. Turn mixture into a shallow, buttered baking dish and bake, uncovered, for 20 minutes at 325°F or until puddinv is firm and browned lightly. Serves 4 to 6.

DONNA'S POTATO DOUGHNUTS

2 cups hot mashed white potatoes
3 tablespoons shortening
1⅔ cups sugar
4 eggs, slightly beaten
2¼ cups milk
⅛ teaspoon salt
⅛ teaspoon nutmeg
½ cup flour
4 teaspoons baking powder
shortening

Mix potatoes, shortening, sugar, and eggs first, then add milk, salt, and nutmeg, blending all thoroughly. Next mix baking powder with flour, then blend flour into mixture thoroughly. Press mix onto floured board and cut into 1- to 2-inch squares. Fry in skillet in hot shortening (about 375°F), turning until golden brown. Makes about 3 dozen doughnuts.

POCATELLO POTATO PUDDING

2 cups mashed potatoes, cooled
1½ cups milk
¼ pound melted butter or margarine
⅔ cup sugar
3 egg yolks, beaten
½ teaspoon lemon juice
dash nutmeg
dash salt
3 egg whites, beaten
3 tablespoons sugar
¼ teaspoon vanilla
¼ teaspoon lemon juice

Soften the mashed potatoes with the milk, then blend in butter, sugar, egg yolks, lemon juice, and salt. Pour mixture into a buttered baking dish and bake at 325°F for about 20 minutes or until pudding is set and top is browned lightly; remove from oven and allow to cool for a few minutes. Beat egg whites, then fold in sugar, vanilla, and lemon juice. Pour meringue mix over pudding, return to oven, and bake another 15 minutes at 325°F or until top is browned. Serves 4 to 6.

ONE-STEP PUMPKIN CUSTARD
1 ¼ cups pumpkin, pared, cooked, strained, and cooled
1 teaspoon softened butter or margarine
1 teaspoon salt
1 cup sugar
1 teaspoon cinnamon
⅛ teaspoon ginger
3 eggs, beaten slightly

Mix pumpkin and milk, then blend in all ingredients except eggs; blend in eggs last, then pour mixture into shallow baking dish and bake, uncovered, for 25 minutes at 325°F or until firm (test with a knife blade: when blade comes clean, custard is done). **Note:** best when served cold. Serves 6 to 8.

MOM'S PUMPKIN PIE
1 ½ cups pumpkin, pared, cooked, and strained
3 egg yolks
1 cup scalded milk
2 tablespoons butter or margarine
1 cup sugar
½ teaspoon salt
¼ teaspoon nutmeg
1 teaspoon ginger
3 egg whites, beaten stiff
pastry for bottom of 9-inch pie pan

Mix all ingredients in a bowl except the egg whites; when mixture is blended thoroughly, add egg whites and mix until smooth. Pour mixture into pastry-lined piepan and bake at 350°F for 40 minutes or until knife blade comes out clean.

SCRUMPTIOUS SQUASH CUSTARD
Same procedure and ingredients as for Pumpkin Custard, except substitute 1 ¼ cups pared, cooked, strained, and cooled acorn or hubbard squash.

ROYAL RHUBARB BREAD PUDDING

2 cups rhubarb, peeled and diced
8 pieces white bread, buttered on one side
1 teaspoon lemon juice
6 tablespoons sugar

Place 4 pieces of buttered bread in the bottom of a buttered 10-inch baking dish. Next, layer the bread with about 1 inch of the diced rhubarb, then sprinkle with half the lemon juice and 2 tablespoons of the sugar. Layer next with 4 slices of bread, remainder of rhubarb, lemon juice, and sugar. Bake, covered, for 25 minutes at 350°F; lower oven temperature to 300°F, remove cover, and continue baking until browned, about 25 minutes. Serves 4 to 6.

RHUBARB PIE

2 cups tender rhubarb, cut into 1-inch pieces
1¼ cups sugar
1 egg, beaten lightly
1 tablespoon flour
pastry for bottom of 9-inch piepan and strips for top

First add sugar to egg and beat well, then add flour and mix thoroughly. Mix sugar-egg mixture with rhubarb, then pour into pastry-lined pie pan; crisscross with strips of dough. Bake for 20 minutes at 400°F, then reduce heat to 350°F and bake another 25 minutes.

CROOKED-NECK PIE

1 cup summer squash, sliced and steamed (crooked-neck squash
     preferred)
3 eggs, beaten
1 cup sugar
1 cup heavy cream
1 teaspoon cinnamon
½ teaspoon nutmeg
½ teaspoon salt
½ teaspoon ginger
pastry for bottom of 9-inch piepan

Strain the steamed squash and set it aside to cool. Add sugar and spices to the squash and mix thoroughly; next add eggs and cream to squash mixture and mix thoroughly. Pour mixture into pastry-lined piepan and bake at 350°F for 40 minutes or until knife blade comes out clean.

SWEET POTATO SAVORIES

1 cup sweet potatoes, pared, cooked, mashed, and cooled
1 tablespoon flour
1 tablespoon sugar
1 egg, beaten
vegetable oil for frying
confectioners' sugar

Mix sweet potatoes, flour, and sugar first, then add egg and mix thoroughly. Form into small balls no larger than 1 inch in diameter. Drop balls into hot vegetable oil (at least 350°F), turning them frequently, and fry them until they are golden brown; drain on absorbent paper. Sprinkle with confectioners' sugar and serve hot. Makes 2 to 3 dozen balls.

SWEET POTATO PUDDING

3 cups sweet potatoes, grated
¼ pound butter or margarine
4 eggs
2 cups sugar
2 cups milk
1 teaspoon salt
dash nutmeg
¼ teaspoon cinnamon

Mix all ingredients together except butter and 1 cup milk. In a skillet over low heat, melt the butter, then add sweet potato mixture, stirring constantly; as mixture thickens, raise heat to medium and add remainder of milk, stirring constantly, and cook for another 5 minutes. Turn mixture into a shallow, buttered baking dish and bake, uncovered, 25 minutea at 325°F or until browned. Serves 6 to 8.

SWEET POTATO PIE

3 cups sweet potatoes, cooked, pared, sliced in ¼-inch slices, and cooled
¼ cup plus 1 tablespoon butter or margarine
1⅓ cups sugar
1 tablespoon allspice
½ teaspoon lemon juice
dash nutmeg
dash cinnamon
pastry for bottom and top of 9-inch piepan

Melt butter in a saucepan over low heat, then blend in sugar, allspice, and lemon juice. Begin layering sweet potato slices in the bottom of the piepan, pouring a small part of the syrupy butter–sugar mixture over each layer; continue until pan is full. Sprinkle nutmeg and cinnamon on top layer, then cover with top layer of pastry. Bake in 350°F oven for 25 to 30 minutes until crust is browned lightly.

BAYOU TOMATO PIE

3 cups green tomatoes, thinly sliced
½ cup melted butter or margarine
¾ cup sugar
1 teaspoon nutmeg
2 tablespoons vinegar
2 tablespoons flour
pastry for bottom and top of 9-inch piepan

In the bottom of the pastry-lined piepan, begin layering the thinly sliced tomatoes. When pan is half full of tomatoes, sprinkle with ¼ cup melted butter, ¼ cup sugar, ½ teaspoon nutmeg, and 1 tablespoon vinegar. Continue layering tomatoes until all are used, then sprinkle the top of the second layer with the remainder of the butter, sugar, nutmeg, and vinegar; sprinkle the flour over this top layer, cover all with pie pastry, and bake in a preheated oven 40 minutes at 375°F or until top is browned. Serve hot or cold.

CANNING
AND
PICKLING VEGETABLES

Many vegetables can be frozen successfully, but methods vary with each type of freezing container and freezing space in most households is usually quite limited. So, for long periods of time, pickling and canning are the two best methods. Equally important, however, is short-term vegetable preservation.

REFRIGERATOR STORAGE

Vegetables can be stored in the vegetable crisper or sealed plastic bags in the refrigerator from one to two weeks. This short-term storage method, however, should be attempted with only the freshest vegetables. For most vegetables, wash, trim, drain, and dry before sealing in plastic bags or putting in crisper. For herbs, salad greens, and all leafy vegetables, trim the roots, soak in colds water for 10 minutes to remove grit, drain, shake off any remaining water, and drain one final time on paper toweling or clean dish towels before refrigerating.

EASY STORAGE

This method involves virtually no work and will keep vegetables for up to three months, sometimes even longer. Storage should be in a cool, dark place: a small room in the cellar, a closet off the kitchen, or a root cellar. The temperature must never be below freezing nor any higher than 50°F; 40°F is ideal. In addition, the area should be free of excess moisture.

Pick vegetables to be stored this way only on sunny, dry days, never after a rain. Again, use only the best of vegetables, those that are free of blemishes, bruises, and insect damage. Never wash vegetables when using this method (they will be washed when taken out of storage, just before cooking).

Wrap each vegetable individually in tissue paper. Wrap firmly, being certain that the vegetable is completely covered. The vegetables can then be stored in baskets, crocks, crates, or even cardboard boxes, but only one variety of vegetable should be stored in each container. You may put containers of several varieties of vegetables in the same area, but if you decide to store fruits using this method, you should store them in a separate area altogether.

Check on the condition of the vegetables once a week. Do not store more of any vegetable than you can reasonably expect to use in a 2- to 3-month period. Tomatoes can be stored while green and placed on windowsills weeks later, after unwrapped, to ripen. We have managed to have ripe, red tomatoes from our garden in the dead of winter by using this method.

GENERAL PICKLING AND CANNING NOTES

For success in preserving vegetables, whether pickling or canning, always observe these general rules.

1. Label jars. Before jars are put away on shelves, affix gummed or self-sticking labels which should include the date the food was preserved, the contents, and any special reminders (e.g., "Extra Sour," "With Garlic").

2. Store canned and pickled goods in a cool, dark, dry place (be wary

of closets too near the kitchen stove). Be certain that the room or closet you select cannot freeze.

3. Choose prime vegetables for both pickling and canning. Make certain vegetables are unbruised, unblemished, and not undergrown or over-ripe. Do not harvest vegetables for preserving until absolutely necessary and never more than 24 hours in advance.

4. Always work fast. Before you begin, have all utensils and equipment set out and ready to use.

5. Use good utensils. You don't have to go out and buy everything new, but do not use any containers or utensils that are cracked, chipped, broken, or grazed.

6. All equipment should be scrupulously clean and free of grease and dust.

7. Wash vegetables several times before beginning any processing steps.

8. After vegetables are canned or pickled and are stored, check them at least once a week. If a lid on a jar is bulging or there is marked discoloration, leakage, or signs of fermentation, discard it. Never eat or taste a vegetable to test it. In fact, if there is any sign which leads you to believe a jar of your preserves might be spoiled, discard the contents at once.

PICKLING

There are two very good reasons why pickling as a food preservation process has been popular for generations. First, the process imparts a truly unique flavor to foods—one which is loved by just about everyone. Second, if the cook is well organized, the procedure itself can be relatively simple.

What You'll Need

1. Soft water. If you have hard water, you can either use distilled water or process your tap water for pickling yourself. To accomplish the latter, add 1 teaspoon of baking soda to 1 gallon of water, boil for 20 minutes, then let the water stand at least 24 hours. Transfer the boiled water to a second container carefully, being certain not to remove the sediment which will collect at the bottom.

2. Pickling salt, which is available in most grocery stores and supermarkets and is clearly labeled as such. *There is no substitute for this.*

3. Vinegar which is of 5% acidity. Most vinegars are this, but check the label. Avoid homemade vinegars. White vinegars preserve the colors of vegetables; red or cider vinegars will darken vegetables but impart a richer flavor.

4. A long-handled stainless, enamelled, or wooden spoon is needed for moving the pickles.

5. Fresh, whole spices. Do not substitute ground spices.

6. Small cloth bags with drawstrings to hold spices inside the jars.

7. Jars (quarts and/or pints, depending on the amounts you intend to preserve) should be unflawed and completely clean and sterilized by boiling water for 10 minutes.

8. Lids should be new, of a type approved for pickling, and the exact match for the type of jars you use.

9. For brining, use stoneware, pottery or glass containers.

10. For pickling, use stainless steel or enamel containers.

Basic Pickling Procedure

Many pickling methods require rather lengthy procedures. This method, however, will yield excellent results in a relatively short period of time as long as you follow each step carefully.

The best vegetables for pickling are cucumber pickles (never remove the entire stem; leave about ⅛ inch), regular cucumbers, carrots, green tomatoes, beans (yellow or green), and onions. Also suitable for pickling are asparagus (only young, thin spears, though), beets, eggplants, sweet peppers, and zucchini.

1. Scrub and wash vegetables extremely well, since any dirt remaining on vegetables can cause bacteria later. Drain vegetables well.

2. In the container to be used for brining, prepare a 10% brine solution. This is done by dissolving, then stirring until well mixed, 1½ cups of pickling salt per 1 gallon of soft or distilled water. (The amount of brine solution you prepare will depend on the number, and size, of the brining containers.) **Note:** the brine solution can be re-used, but each time vegetables are brined the strength of the mixture becomes diminished. For this reason, it is best to use brining solutions only twice. The second time the brine is used, it should be replenished by adding 3 heaping tablespoons of pickling salt to each gallon of water.

3. Place vegetables to be pickled in the brine solution, being certain that there is enough liquid to cover vegetables completely. (Cherry or grape leaves, as long as they haven't been sprayed, will help make pickled vegetables crisp. Wash them well, then interlayer them with the vegetables for the brining process. Discard them when transferring vegetables from the brine.) Let vegetables stand in brine for the time period called for in the recipe —usually from 12 to 24 hours.

4. Drain the vegetables, rinse with clear water, then drain again.

5. Place vegetables in sterile jars. Place whole vegetables or parts in jars, but do not pack too tightly.

6. Boil the pickling solution, then, using a jar funnel, fill jars with pickling solution to ¼ inch from the top of the rim.

7. Wipe the jar rims with a clean cloth, then seal the jars with the proper lids.

8. Using either a pressure canner with the petcock left completely open or a conventional hot-water canner, boil the jars. **Note:** whatever type utensil is used, a rack is necessary on the bottom, to keep jars from cracking from direct contact with heat. Fill the container about halfway with boiling water, then, using a jar lifter or canning tongs, lower the packed, sealed jars into the water, being certain that the jars do not touch one another. A good rule is to leave 1½ to 2½ inches of space between the jars. Pour on boiling water until the jar tops are at least 2 inches under

water. *Do not pour water directly on jars.* Heat until boiling rapidly, then cover the canner with a lid and process for 15 minutes.

9. Turn off the heat, remove the cover, then, using a jar lifter or canning tongs, lift the jars from the water, being careful not to lift jars by their lids.

10. Put the jars on cloth or several layers of paper toweling, letting them stand until completely dry and cool. Labels can be put on jars once they're dry.

Recipes

GREEN TOMATO PICKLES

16 quarts green tomatoes, cut in halves, quarters, or eighths
6 large onions, peeled and sliced
2 cups pickling salt
1½ gallons cider vinegar
2 tablespoons salt
6 sweet peppers (green, red, or a mixture), seeded and cut into eighths
3 tablespoons dry mustard
6 pounds brown sugar*
3 tablespoons whole cloves
3 tablespoons powdered ginger
2 tablespoons celery seed

*For more tart green tomato pickles, use 3 pounds of brown sugar.

Sprinkle pickling salt over green tomatoes and onions, stir a few times, then refrigerate. After 12 hours, rinse with clear water and drain well. Heat vinegar to a boil, then add salt, sweet peppers, dry mustard, and brown sugar. After 5 minutes of boiling, add tomatoes and onions. Put cloves, ginger and celery seed in a cloth bag, then add to mixture. With spice bag immersed, simmer 1¼ hours, stirring often. Remove spice bag. Transfer pickles, peppers, and onions to sterile jars, adding enough liquid to fill jars to ¼ inch from top of rims. Seal jars, then give them the boiling water bath for 15 minutes. Yields 12 quarts or 24 pints.

PICKLED BEANS

4 pounds green beans with stems removed
8 cloves garlic
8 dill heads or 8 tablespoons dill seed
5 cups water
5 cups vinegar
⅔ cup salt

Place the beans lengthwise in 8 sterile pint jars. Add 1 garlic clove and 1 dill head or 1 tablespoon dill seed to each jar. Boil the water, vinegar and salt together, stirring once, then pour over the beans, filling to ¼ inch from top of rims. Seal jars, then give them the boiling water bath for 15 minutes. Yields 8 pints.

PICKLED CARROTS

3 pounds carrots, peeled and sliced into pieces 3 inches long and
   no wider than ½ inch
2¼ cups vinegar
2¼ cups water
1¼ cups sugar
1 tablespoon mixed pickling spices, whole

In boiling water, cook carrots until just tender, 8 to 10 minutes only. Boil vinegar, water, sugar, and spices. Drain carrots, then pack in sterile quart or pint jars (leave about 1 inch of room below rim). Pour hot pickling solution into jars, then seal and give jars the boiling water bath for 15 minutes. Yields 3 quarts or 6 pints.

PICKLED ONIONS

8 quarts white onions, peeled
2 gallons water
3 cups pickling salt
1 gallon white vinegar
3 cups sugar
3 bay leaves

Mix 10% brine solution with water and pickling salt, then place peeled onions in solution; brine onions 24 hours, refrigerated. Drain, then rinse well and drain again. Mix vinegar and sugar and bring to a boil, then add onions; reduce heat and simmer 5 minutes. Place onions in jars, then pour on vinegar solution. In each jar, place ½ to ¼ bay leaf. Seal and give jars the boiling water bath for 30 minutes. Yields 6 quarts or 12 pints.

PICKLED ZUCCHINI

5 pounds small zucchini, unpeeled but stems removed, sliced
    lengthwise into ¼-inch slices
6 small white onions, peeled and sliced
⅔ cup pickling salt
6 cups cider vinegar
1 tablespoon mustard seed
1 tablespoon celery seed
2½ cups sugar

Place zucchini and onions in container and pour on only enough cold water to cover. Then sprinkle on pickling salt, stir once, and let stand for 2½ hours. Drain well. Bring vinegar, mustard seed, celery seed, and sugar to a boil; boil 3 minutes, stirring frequently. Remove vinegar solution from heat, then add zucchini and onions, letting mixture stand for 2 hours. Return to heat and boil 4 minutes. Remove from heat, pack zucchini and onions in aterile jars, then pour hot vinegar solution into jars. Seal and give jars the boiling water bath for 15 minutes. Yields 3 quarts or 6 pints.

SWEET AND SOUR PICKLES

10 pounds cucumber pickles
½ cup pickling salt
7 cups water
2 quarts cider vinegar
5 cups sugar
1 tablespoon mixed pickling spices
½ teaspoon cloves
6 peppercorns

Combine pickling salt and water, then add pickles and soak for 24 hours. After pickles are removed from the brine solution, pour enough boiling, clear water over them to cover, let stand 1 minute, then drain well. Place pickles in sterilized jars. Bring vinegar, sugar, pickling spices, cloves, and peppercorns — all in a cloth bag — to the boiling point, then pour entire mixture into jars, discarding spice bag. Seal and give jars the boiling water bath for 15 minutes. Yields 12 pints.

Note: Store pickled goods at least 4 weeks before using them, preferably 6 weeks. The flavor of pickled vegetables improves markedly if allowed to stand for this period.

DILL PICKLES

8 pounds cucumber pickles
6 cups white vinegar
6 cups water
⅔ cup pickling salt
24 garlic cloves, peeled and halved
18-20 tablespoons dill seed
30 peppercorns

Mix vinegar, water, and pickling salt in a large kettle and begin to heat. Add garlic cloves, stir, and bring mixture to a boil. When rapid boiling begins, remove garlic and discard. Place cucumbers in sterile quart jars. To each jar, add 3 generous tablespoons of dill seed and 5 peppercorns. Pour hot pickling liquid into jars, leaving ½ to ¼ inches of room below rim. Seal and give jars the boiling water bath for 15 minutes. Yields 6 quarts.

CANNING

It is best to begin the section on canning with a cautionary note. Clostridium botulinum, the sometimes lethal germ, can thrive in nonacid canned food even though the food has not suffered any change in color or odor. Even when not deadly, botulism causes severe stomach pains, vomiting, coughing, visual irregularities, and muscular weakness. When canning, you must use extreme caution in every step of the canning process. Even when you have completed your canning work and are prepared to begin using your canned goods, there is one additional step you should adhere to: boil all nonacid vegetables, uncovered, for 15 minutes—not a minute less—before serving. You should also stir the vegetables often while cooking. The Department of Agriculture advises that cabbage, cauliflower, celery, cucumbers, eggplant, lettuce, onions, parsnips, turnips, or any mixtures of vegetables not be canned at home.

What You'll Need
    1. Jars. Do not use ordinary jars. Use only approved canning jars, unflawed and sterilized. **Note:** Jars must be able to withstand heats of 240°F or more.
    2. Lids. Be certain you have the proper, matching lids for your jars. We recommend only the types of lids which have the rubber seal built into them. They must be clean, but it is not advisable to boil them. They should be washed with soap, rinsed completely, and placed in a pan with water to cover; bring the water to a simmer—do not boil. After heating, leave the lids in the water until it is time to use them.
    3. Clean, sterilized utensils for transferring vegetables.
    4. A pressure canner. This is the most efficient, safest method for canning vegetables. Jars of vegetables should be canned at 240°F and 10 pounds of pressure. **Note:** Air must be vented from the pressure-canner for

at least 10 minutes before the petcock is closed. After it is closed, the pressure must be raised to 10 pounds. The time of processing should not be started *until* pressure reaches 10 pounds.

Basic Canning Procedure

1. Thoroughly wash the vegetables you plan to can. Pare vegetables if necessary. Cut and/or slice into the same size pieces you would if you were preparing to serve right away.

2. Vegetables to be canned should be pre-cooked before being put into jars. To do this, bring water to a boil. Then, with vegetables in a metal cooking basket, immerse them in the boiling water. Do not count precooking time until the water recovers its boil again. After removing the cooking basket from the boiling water, plunge it into cold water, lift it out immediately, then immerse it once again. **Note:** Save the vitamin-rich water from precooking to fill canning jars.

3. Pack hot, sterilized jars with precooked vegetables, always leaving at least ¾ inch of room between the top of the vegetables and the jar rim. **Note:** corn, lima beans, and peas swell, so leave from 1 to 1¼ inch of room between the top of the vegetables and the jar rim.

4. Using a jar funnel, pour boiling liquid—the precooking water—over the produce in the jars to cover, leaving some room above the level of the liquid and the jar rim.

5. Using a long-bladed knife, insert the blade along the inside of the jar, then turn the packed produce slightly, shifting its position and releasing air bubbles. Using a clean cloth, wipe the jar rims carefully, then put on the lids.

6. Place the jars in a pressure canner, leaving space between them. After the pressure canner has been vented, process for proper amount of time.

7. Take the pressure canner from the heat, set it on a rack, and allow the pressure to return to zero before the lid is removed. Then use a jar lifter or canning tongs to remove the jars from canner.

8. Set the upright jars in a place where they can remain undisturbed for at least 12 hours.

9. After the jars have sat, check to see if the lids have made a proper seal with the jars. Using a metal spoon, tap the lids just lightly—and just one tap per lid. If you hear a clear, ringing sound, the seal on the jar is good. If the sound you get from your tapping seems dull and hollow, do not store the food in the canned state; instead, use it as soon as possible.

10. The jars of canned goods are now ready for storage. Label each jar, then store it in a dark place which has some circulation of air and where the temperature remains between 45° and 60°F—55°F is ideal.

Vegetable	Preparation	Precooking Time	Room Between Liquid and Jar Rim	Processing Time in Pressure Canner at 10 Pounds Pressure
Asparagus	cut away loose scales and ends; cut into 2-inch pieces	2 minutes	½ inch	30 minutes
Beans, green or wax	cut off tips; cut into 1-inch pieces	4 minutes	½ inch	25 minutes
Beans, lima	shell beans from pods	4 minutes	1 inch	50 minutes
Beets	peel, remove stems and roots; cut into pieces	10 minutes	½ inch	35 minutes
Carrots	scrape off skins, remove stems; cut into 2-inch pieces	4 minutes	1 inch	30 minutes
Corn	remove kernels from cob	for each qt. of corn, use 2¼ cups boiling water; bring to a boil; put in jars	1 inch PACK HOT	80 minutes

			at once, not adding any additional water	
Greens (not lettuce)	wash several times; discard discolored leaves or stalks; cut into small pieces	5 minutes in 1 or 2 inches of water, covered, until wilted	1 inch PACK HOT	85 minutes
Okra	cut off stem caps, but do not cut into pod	3 minutes in boiling water to cover	1 inch PACK HOT	40 minutes
Peas	shell peas from pods	3 minutes in boiling water to cover	1 inch USE PINTS ONLY	40 minutes
Peppers, green	cut away stems, seeds, and membranes; quarter	2 minutes	½ inch ADD 1 teaspoon lemon juice to each quart	35 minutes
Potatoes, white	remove skins; cut into pieces	8 minutes in boiling water to cover	1 inch ADD ½ teaspoon salt to each quart	40 minutes

141

Vegetable	Preparation	Precooking Time	Room Between Liquid and Jar Rim	Processing Time in Pressure Canner at 10 Pounds Pressure
Pumpkins and winter squash	remove skins; cut into small pieces	cook, covered, until tender; then push through food mill or put in blender	1 inch PACK HOT	75 minutes
Summer squash	cut away ends; cut into small pieces	3 minutes in boiling water to cover	½ inch	40 minutes
Sweet potatoes	remove skins; cut into small pieces	10 minutes	1 inch USE FRESH WATER	90 minutes
Tomatoes	drop into boiling water for 1 minute; plunge into cold water; remove skins; cut into quarters		½ inch Use BOILING WATER OR BOILING TO-MATO JUICE	10 minutes

My Special Recipes and Hints

My Special Recipes and Hints

My Special Recipes and Hints

My Special Recipes and Hints

My Special Recipes and Hints

My Special Recipes and Hints

My Special Recipes and Hints

My Special Recipes and Hints

My Special Recipes and Hints

INDEX